UTOPIAS, DOLPHINS AND COMPUTERS

OTHER BOOKS BY MARY MIDGLEY

UTOPIAS, DOLPHINS AND COMPUTERS

Problems of Philosophical Plumbing

Mary Midgley

London and New York

First published 1996
by Routledge
11 New Fetter Lane, London EC4P 4EE

Simultaneously published in the USA and Canada
by Routledge
29 West 35th Street, New York, NY 10001

Reprinted 1996

Typeset in Galliard by
Florencetype Limited, Stoodleigh, Devon

Printed and bound in Great Britain by
Biddles Short Run Books, King's Lynn.

British Library Cataloguing in Publication Data
A catalogue record for this book is available from the British Library.

Library of Congress Cataloging in Publication Data
Midgely, Mary, 1919–
Utopias, dolphins, and computers: some problems in philosophical
plumbing/Mary Midgley.
p. cm.
Includes bibliographical references.
1. Philosophy.   2. Man.   3. Applied ethics.   4. Animals.
I. Title.
B1647.M473U76   1996
100–dc20   96–5494
                                                      CIP

ISBN 0–415–13377–7

CONTENTS

For James Lovelock
More power to his elbow!

FOREWORD

This is one book although its chapters were originally written as separate papers. Its theme has two sides. On the one hand I discuss the huge difficulties which we experience in trying to theorize about the world – some of them timeless, unavoidable difficulties, some sharply contemporary. On the other hand, I point to certain special aspects of our present world where I think philosophy is badly needed and can be really helpful – aspects such as the position of women and that of animals, the state of the environment, the plurality of cultures, the meaning of artificial intelligence.

The earlier chapters of this book concentrate more on the inner, philosophical difficulties, the later ones more on the outward aspect, the current state of these particular topics in the world. But throughout I have tried to develop the two concerns together so as to make them illuminate one another as much as possible. I have brought these papers together in order to do this, since they seemed to me to contain points which made more sense together than they might seem to do apart. They have been chosen with this aim in mind and I have revised them thoroughly so as to bring out links between them and to shape a common theme.

Although most of the papers have appeared somewhere before, they have done so in the most diverse places and some of them would now be quite hard to find. I must therefore thank the various editors and publishers responsible, for their earlier hospitality and for giving permission to reprint these pieces. Their original sites were as follows:

'Philosophical Plumbing' appeared in *The Impulse to Philosophize* (edited by A. Phillips Griffiths, Cambridge University Press 1992).
'Practical Utopianism' in *The Right to Hope, Global Problems, Global Visions* (edited by Catherine Thick, Earthscan Publications, 1995).

'Homunculus Trouble' in the *Journal of Social Philosophy* (San Antonio, Texas) vol. 21, no. 1, Spring 1991.

'Myths of Intellectual Isolation' in *Proceedings of the Aristotelian Society*, vol. 89, part 1, 1988–9.

'The Use and Uselessness of Learning' in *The European Journal of Education* (Oxford), vol. 25, no. 3, 1990.

'Sex and Personal Identity' in *Encounter*, 63 (June 1984), pp. 50–5.

'Freedom, Feminism and War' in *African Philosophical Enquiry* (Ibadan, Nigeria), vol. 1, no. 2, July 1987.

'The End of Anthropocentrism?' in *Philosophy and the Natural Environment* (ed. Robin Attfield and Andrew Belsey, Cambridge University Press, 1994).

'Is a Dolphin a Person?' appeared under the title 'Persons and Non-Persons' in *In Defence of Animals* (ed. Peter Singer, Oxford, Basil Blackwell, 1985).

'Sustainability and Moral Pluralism' was originally written for the IUCN. A version of it appeared in *Ethics and the Environment* (Athens, GA), vol. 1, no. 1, 1996.

'Visions: Secular, Sacred and Scientific' appeared under the title 'Visions, Secular and Sacred' in the *Hastings Center Report* (Briarcliff Manor, NY) for September–October 1995.

'Creativity and Artificial Intelligence' has not been previously published.

1

PHILOSOPHICAL PLUMBING

— ·◆· —

WATER AND THOUGHT

IS PHILOSOPHY like plumbing? I have made this comparison a number of times, wanting to stress that philosophizing is not just grand and elegant and difficult, it is also needed. It isn't optional. The idea caused mild surprise, and has sometimes been thought rather undignified. The question of dignity is a very interesting one, to which we will come back at the end of this chapter. But first, I would like to work the comparison out a bit more fully.

Plumbing and philosophy are both activities that arise because elaborate cultures like ours have, beneath their surface, a fairly complex system which is usually unnoticed, but which sometimes goes wrong. In both cases, this can have serious consequences. Each system supplies vital needs for those who live above it. Each is hard to repair when it does go wrong, because neither of them was ever consciously planned as a whole. There have been many ambitious attempts to reshape both of them. But, for both, existing complications are usually too widespread to allow a completely new start.

Neither system ever had a single designer who knew exactly what needs it would have to meet. Instead, both have grown imperceptibly over the centuries in the sort of way that organisms grow, and are constantly being altered piecemeal to suit changing demands as the ways of life above them have branched out. Both are therefore now very intricate. When trouble arises, specialized skill is needed if there is to be any hope of locating it and putting it right.

Here, however, we run into the first striking difference between the two cases. About plumbing, everybody accepts this need for trained specialists. About philosophy, many people – especially British people – not only doubt the need, they are often sceptical about whether the underlying system even exists at all. It is much more deeply hidden. When the concepts we are living by work badly, they don't usually

1

drip audibly through the ceiling or swamp the kitchen floor. They just quietly distort and obstruct our thinking.

We often don't consciously notice this obscure malfunction, any more than we consciously notice the discomfort of an unvarying bad smell or of a cold that creeps on gradually. We may indeed complain that life is going badly – that our actions and relationships are not turning out as we intend. But it can be very hard to see why this is happening, or what to do about it. We find it much easier to look for the source of trouble outside ourselves than within. Notoriously, it is hard to see faults in our own motivation, in the structure of our feelings. But it is in some ways even harder – even less natural – to turn our attention to what might be wrong in the structure of our thought. Attention naturally flows outwards to faults in the world around us. Bending thought round to look critically at itself is quite hard. That is why, in any culture, philosophy is a relatively late development.

When things do go badly, however, we have to do this. We must then somehow readjust our underlying concepts; we must shift the set of assumptions that we were brought up with. We must restate those existing assumptions – which are normally muddled and inarticulate – so as to find the source of trouble. And this new statement must somehow be put in a usable form, a form which makes the necessary changes look possible.

QUARRELS BETWEEN PHILOSOPHY AND POETRY?

That need to readjust our concepts is the need that philosophy exists to satisfy. It is *not* just a need felt by highly educated people. It is a need that can spoil the lives even of people with little interest in thinking, and its pressure can be vaguely felt by anyone who tries to think at all. As that pressure becomes fiercer, people who are determined to think particularly hard do sometimes manage to devise a remedy for this obscure discomfort, and this is how philosophy first got started. Time and again in the past, when conceptual schemes have begun to work badly, someone has contrived to suggest a change that shifts the blockage, allowing thought to flow where it is needed.

Once this has happened, the bystanders tend to heave deep sighs and say, 'Aha – of course, I knew that all along. Why didn't I happen to say it before?' (Sometimes indeed they think that they have done so . . .) These new suggestions usually come in part from sages who are not full-time philosophers, notably from poetry and other arts. Shelley was right to say that poets are among the unacknowledged legislators of mankind. They can show us the new vision. But to work the new ideas out fully is still a different kind of work. Whoever does it, it is always philosophical business. It needs, not just a new vision, but also the thorough, disciplined articulation of its details and consequences.

Much of this work is boring, and it can sometimes prove astonishingly long and difficult, but it is indispensable. Any powerful new idea calls for a great deal of change, and the more useful that idea is going to be, the more need there is to work out these changes fully. For doing this, it really is very helpful to be acquainted with other visions and other sets of changes, to have some background training in the way that past conceptual developments have worked. Of course there have been some self-educated philosophers who didn't have the advantage of this background – Tom Paine was one – but the work is much harder for them.

Great philosophers, then, need a combination of gifts that is rare. They must be lawyers as well as poets. They must have both the new vision that points the way we are to go and the logical doggedness that sorts out just what is, and what is not, involved in going there. It is this difficult balancing act that has gained them a respect which is different from the respect due to either kind of work on its own. It accounts for the peculiar prestige which philosophy still has, even among people who are extremely vague about what it is or why they might need it.

Keeping these two functions together is hard. Where philosophy is salaried and professionalized, the lawyer-like skills are almost bound to predominate because you can examine people to test their logical competence and industry, but you can't test their creativity. These skills are then no longer being used to clarify any specially important new vision. Philosophy becomes scholastic, a specialized concern for skilled plumbers doing fine plumbing, and sometimes doing it on their own in laboratories. This happened in the late Middle Ages; it seems to have happened in China, and it has happened to Anglo-American philosophy during much of this century.

THE VISION THING

This self-contained, scholastic philosophy remains an impressive feat, something which may be well worth doing for its own sake. It is quite right that there should be deeply specialized thought, like some mathematics (for example) that most of us cannot penetrate at all. But if philosophers treat this esoteric area as their central business, they leave a most dangerous gap in the intellectual scene. This work cannot, of course, stop the other aspect, the visionary aspect of philosophy, from being needed, nor that need from being supplied. The hungry sheep who don't get that creative vision look up and are not fed. They tend to wander round looking for new visions until they find some elsewhere. Thus, a good deal of visionary philosophizing has been imported lately from Europe and from the East, from the social sciences, from evangelists, from literary criticism and from science fiction, as well as from past philosophers. But it doesn't necessarily bring with it the disciplined, detailed thinking that is needed to apply it to life.

The living water flows in, but it is not channelled to where it is needed. It seeps around, often forming floods, and it finally settles in pools where chance dictates, because the local philosophic practitioners won't attend to it. In fact, the presence of these alien streams often merely exasperates them. They suspect that the public has no business to ask for visions at all, and that unlicensed merchants have certainly no business to supply them.

So we get a new version of the old 'quarrel between philosophy and poetry' that Plato worried about in the *Republic*, a demarcation dispute embittered by modern professional territorialism and academic specialization. Philosophers are tempted to imitate other academic specialists by defensively narrowing their subject. They follow the specialized scientists, who claim that nothing counts as 'science' except the negative results of control-experiments performed inside laboratories, and the specialized historians, who insist that only value-free, non-interpreted bits of information can count as history. Ignoring the philosophic howlers that are so obvious in these claims, these philosophers in their turn also rule that only technical, purely formal work, published in learned journals and directed at their colleagues, can count as 'philosophy'.

Do they still do this? Much less so, I think, than they did a little time back. In the last few decades, many people have indeed noticed the absurdity of over-specialization, the emptiness of the heavily defended academic fortress. But unfortunately, these absurdities are built into hiring-and-firing and promotion procedures that will take a long time to change, even when the need for change is widely understood. Meanwhile, it needs to be loudly and often said that this contracting of territories, this defensive demarcation-disputing among professionals, is not just misguided. It is pernicious and thoroughly unprofessional.

Learning is not a private playground for the learned. It is something that belongs to, and affects, all of us. Because we are a culture that values knowledge and understanding so highly, the part of every study that can be widely understood – the general, interpretative part, the ideology – always does seep out in the end and concern us all. The conceptual schemes used in every study are not private ponds; they are streams that are fed from our everyday thinking, are altered by the learned, and eventually flow back into it, influencing our lives.

This is not true only of philosophy. In history, for instance, ideas about the nature of social causation, about the importance or unimportance of individual acts or of economic and social factors, are constantly changing. Historians can't actually be neutral about these things, because they have to pick out what they think worth investigating. Selection always shows bias, and must have its eventual influence. All that specialist scholars gain by refusing to attend to this bit of philosophy is ignorance about their own thinking, ignorance of their own commitment and of the responsibility it carries. The same thing is true of science. One has only to think of the part that concepts like 'relativity' or 'evolution' have played in our everyday thought during the twentieth century to see this.

But of course, philosophy is the key case, because it is the study whose peculiar business it is to concentrate on the gaps between all the others, and to understand the relations between them. Conceptual schemes as such are philosophy's concern, and these schemes do constantly go wrong. Conceptual confusion is deadly, and a great deal of it afflicts our everyday life. It needs to be seen to, and if the professional philosophers don't look at it, there is no one else whose role it is to do so.

THE SELF-HELP OPTION

Ought we each to be able to do this on our own, on a do-it-yourself basis? This attractive idea probably lies at the heart of British anti-intellectualism. We do sometimes manage this private philosophizing, and there is, of course, a great deal to be said for trying. But it is extremely hard to get started. Indeed, as I mentioned, often we find it hard to imagine that anything definite is wrong with our concepts at all.

This is the crucial paradox. Why are we not more aware of our conceptual needs? The difficulty is that (as I have mentioned), once this kind of work is done, conceptual issues drop out of sight and are forgotten. That is why people have the idea that philosophy has never solved any problems. Systems of ideas which are working smoothly become more or less invisible. (This, of course, is what provoked my original comparison with plumbing, another service for which we are seldom as grateful as we might be). Until they explode, we assume that the ideas we are using are the only ideas that have ever been possible. We think either that everybody uses these ideas or that, if there are people who don't, they are simply unenlightened, 'primitive', misinformed, misguided, wicked or extremely stupid.

EXAMPLE: THE SOCIAL CONTRACT

It is time to mention some examples. But it is tricky finding the right ones. This disregard of our conceptual schemes is so strong, so natural, that in order to pick on an instance of what I am talking about, we need to choose a notion that is already making too much trouble to be disregarded. I considered discussing the Machine Model here, but it is now wallowing in too many kinds of difficulty to deal with at this point. Instead, let us open a related manhole and look at the idea of the Social Contract.

That was the conceptual tool used by prophets of the Enlightenment to explain political obligation from below rather than from above. Instead of saying that kings must be obeyed because they were appointed by God, philosophers suggested that the only reason for obeying any kind of government was that it represented the will of the people governed and served their interests. At last, unsatisfactory kings were expendable. Civic duty sprang only from tacit agreement among rational citizens, each concerned for their own interest – an agreement regularly tested through voting.

After fierce disputes and much bloodshed, this startling idea was quite widely accepted. Once it had become so, questions about it largely ceased to be noticed and vanished under the floorboards of many Western institutions. On the whole, we in the West now take contract thinking for granted, and we are not alone in doing that. The authority of contract is, for instance, treated as obvious by the many oppressed and misgoverned peoples all over the world who are now demanding something called 'democracy'. Yet difficulties about that concept do still arise, and indeed they are on the increase. Lately, distinct patches of dry rot have arisen around it, and there have been some very odd smells.

For instance – if we rely heavily on the notion of contract – we have to ask, what about the interests of non-voting parties? What, for a start, about the claims of children, of the inarticulate and the insane, and of people as yet unborn? What about something that, till recently, our moralists hardly mentioned at all, namely the non-human, non-speaking world – the needs of animals and plants, of the ocean and the Antarctic and the rainforests? There is a whole great range of questions here which we now see to be vital, but which we find strangely hard to deal with, simply because our culture has been so obsessed with models centring on contract. Again, even within the set of possible contractors, we might ask who is entitled to a voice on what? What happens to the interests of people in one democratic country who suffer by the democratically agreed acts of another? What, too, about minorities within a country, minorities who must live by decisions they did not vote for? (A question which Mill worried about profoundly in his *Essay on Liberty*.) And so on.

Plainly, social-contract thinking is no sort of adequate guide for constructing the whole social and political system. It really is a vital means of protection against certain sorts of oppression, an essential defence against tyranny. But it must not be taken for granted and forgotten as a safe basis for all sorts of institutions. It needs always to be seen as something partial and provisional, an image that may cause trouble and have to be altered. It is a tool to be used, not a final decree of fate or an idol to be worshipped. It is, in fact, just one useful analogy among many. It must always be balanced against others which bring out other aspects of the complex truth.

This provisional quality is, in fact, a regular feature of conceptual schemes. None of them is isolated; none of them is safe from the possibility of clashing with others. If they are successful, they always tend to expand and eventually to be used on unsuitable material. (One can see this happening all the time with intellectual fashions). The cluster of ideas that centres on the image of contract has been very expansive, generating powerful ideas of rights, autonomy, interests, competition, rationality as self-interest, and so forth. It has strongly influenced our whole idea of what an individual is – again, something that we take for granted and rarely think to alter when we run into trouble.

THE DESTRUCTIVE SIDE OF INDIVIDUALISM

Contract thinking makes individuals look much more separate than most cultures have taken them to be – more separate, surely, than they actually are. It says that there is really no such thing as society, that the state is only a logical construction out of its members. By contrast with older organic metaphors such as 'we are members one of another', contract-talk portrays people as essentially distinct beings – billiard-balls on the table – each free to make just what contracts it chooses and to abstain from all others.

This individualism is, of course, particularly revolutionary if it is applied to personal relations, and it has been meant to be applied there. The defence of individuals against outside interference has been personal as well as political, seen as a deliberate emancipation from all non-chosen obligations, notably from allegiance to parents and from permanent marriage. Because these institutions really had been used for tyrannous purposes, they too caused alarm. Systematic contract thinking makes it possible to rule that personal relationships, like political ones, can only arise out of freely negotiated contracts, and that what is freely negotiated can at any time be freely annulled.

This conceptual move certainly did make possible much greater social freedom, and thus a great deal of self-fulfilment. Yet it has some extremely odd consequences. Unfortunately, personal relations, such as friendship, do normally have to be relied on to last, because they involve some real joining-together of the parties. Friends share their lives; they are no longer totally separate entities. They are not pieces of Lego that have just been fitted together for convenience.

LEGO IS NOT LIKE LIFE

People are different from Lego. If you have been my friend for years, that friendship has changed both of us. We now rely deeply on each other; we have exchanged some functions, we contain elements of each other's lives. We are quite properly mutually dependent, not because of some shameful weakness, but just in proportion to what we have put into this friendship and what we have made of it. Of course any friendship can end if it has to, but that ending will be a misfortune. It will wound us. An organic model, which says that we are members one of another, describes this situation far better than a Lego model. And what is true of friendship is of course still more true of those personal relationships which are of most importance in forming our lives, namely, our relations to our parents and to our children. We didn't choose either parents or children; we never made a contract with either. Yet we certainly are deeply bound to both.

Is this binding a tragic infringement of our freedom? Some twentieth-century theorists, such as the Existentialists, have said that it is, that any mutual dependence, any merging of individual lives, is bad faith. Freedom itself is (as Sartre told us) the only fixed value, the ideal against which all others must be judged. Here, of course, the

8

concept of freedom itself has been radically reshaped. It appears, no longer just as a necessary condition of pursuing other ideals, but as being itself the only possible ideal. It is not seen as consisting in the ability to do things which we independently know to be important but simply as heroic solitude. In fact, in this vision, freedom itself becomes almost synonymous with solitude, the undisturbed life of the Lego-piece that has retired under the sofa, existing according to its own chosen principles without interference from anyone.

Now, no doubt this is a possible ideal. There are hermits who seem to live by it, though they are not many and, of course, it is not very easy to find out whether that is really what they are doing. But this impregnable solitude is certainly a very *odd* ideal, and there seems no reason why the rest of us ought to adopt it. What has made it look impressive is surely something that very often happens over conceptual schemes. A pattern of ideas has been extended from the political field – where it was quite suitable and successful – into the private one, simply because of its success.

Resistance to tyranny, and resistance to the dead hand of tradition, had proved most relevant causes in the public context. They obviously had some application in the private one as well, so they began to look like an all-purpose remedy there too. Countless parricidal novels were shaped round them, from Samuel Butler's *The Way of All Flesh* and the novels of revolt about the First World War on to the present day. But the negative, destructive aim always needs to be supplemented with something more positive, if people are not simply to give up in despair.

This is what limits the value of the individualistic pattern. It tells us how to reject the bonds that we have – which may be very helpful – but it has not the slightest suggestion to make about what we should look for instead. In actual living, we normally don't follow such negative patterns beyond the rebellions of adolescence, to which indeed they properly belong. Left to ourselves, without moralistic propaganda, we quite quickly find aspects of tradition that are not dead but life-giving, and form new relationships which need not be tyrannous.

But we are not left to ourselves, because the morality of our age runs so strongly in destructive channels more appropriate to politics. Individualistic ideologies can make nothing of these cheerful discoveries about benign traditions and good relationships. They merely denounce them as disgraceful symptoms of moral cowardice, and since we are prone to guilt, we readily try to believe them. We cannot, however, easily find alternative ways of thinking to replace them. Organic models, which would probably help us, have for some time been treated with great suspicion because, on the political scene, they have been misused for the defence of tyranny.

With the rise of concern about the environment, this tabu on organic ways of thinking may now be lifting. It may even become possible for our species to admit that it is not really some supernatural variety of Lego, but a kind of an animal. This ought to make it easier to admit also that we are not self-contained and self-sufficient, either as a species or as individuals, but live naturally in deep mutual dependence. Of course these organic models too will need watching; of course they too can be abused. But if we can once get it into our heads that a model is only a model, if we can grasp the need to keep correcting one model philosophically against another, then some sort of social life begins to look possible again.

NO MODEL IS AN ISLAND

Where is all this taking us?

I have mentioned the social-contract model as an example of the underlying conceptual schemes that we rely on, and I have so far said two things about it: first, that this model is merely an indicator of much wider and deeper structures. It is exceptional in that it is already making visible trouble, so we are more aware of it than we are of many others. What we chiefly need to notice is the unconsidered mass that lies behind it. I am sorry if that sounds like a rather paradoxical demand to notice what one isn't noticing, but really it makes quite good sense – compare it with plumbing. The point is, of course, that we need to remember how large and powerful the hidden system of ideas is, so as to be ready to spot any particular elements of it which do make trouble. Dogmatic empiricists who simply don't believe that powerful thought-systems are there at all really are in a situation much like sceptics who don't believe in the drains and the water supply. The alternative to getting a proper philosophy is not avoiding philosophy altogether, which cannot be done, but continuing to use a bad one.

Second, I have been saying that this social-contract model, like all other such models, is partial and provisional. Even the most useful, the most vital of such patterns of thought, has its limits. They all need to be balanced and corrected against one another. The strong unifying tendency that is natural to our thought keeps making us hope that we have found a single pattern which is a Theory of Everything – a key to all the mysteries, the secret of the universe ... A long series of failures has shown that this can't work. That realization seems to be the sensible element at the core of the conceptual muddle now known as Postmodernism, though it is often obscured by much less useful excursions into the wilder shores of relativism.

This discovery that truth isn't monolithic doesn't really leave us in a sceptical, relativistic welter, because the various patterns overlap and can be related to each other. But it does mean that we need to view *controversy* very differently. An immense proportion of academic time, paper and word-processing power is used on battles between rival models, both of which have their place, instead of on quietly working out what that place is and how to fit them together. Academic imperialism constantly sets up unnecessary tournaments. Attempts at takeover are very common where scholars are not specially trained to avoid them, and of course these attempts are encouraged when there is a vacuum of serious, wider theorizing. Philosophers themselves may no longer insist, as Hegel did, on building systems that explain everything, but sages from other disciplines are still at it.

I am, then, using this parallel with plumbing to say that the patterns underlying our thought are much more powerful, more intricate and more dangerous than we usually notice, that they need constant attention, and that no one of them is a safe universal guide. What more should be said about these patterns? Chiefly, I think, that to understand their power we need to grasp their strong hold on the imagination – their relation to myth.

THE ROLE OF IMAGERY

Myths are stories symbolizing profoundly important patterns, patterns that are very influential but too large, too deep and too imperfectly known to be expressed literally. Sometimes myths are actual stories – narratives – and when they are, these narratives don't, of course, need to be literally true. Thus the social-contract myth tells a story of an agreement that was once arrived at, but no one supposes that this ever actually happened. The story can indeed sometimes be an actual lie, like the forgery of the 'Protocols of the Elders of Zion', and the lie will not be nailed until the essence of the myth – the meaning that has gripped the imagination of myth-bound people – is somehow reached and defused.

Examples like these led Enlightenment thinkers to denounce all myths and to proclaim, in positivistic style, a new age free from symbols, an age when all thoughts would be expressed literally, language being used only to report scientific facts. But the notion of such an age is itself a highly fanciful myth, an image quite unrelated to the way in which thought and language really work. The idea of dispensing with symbols is a doomed one. All our thinking works through them. New ideas commonly occur to us first as images and are expressed first as metaphors. Even in talking about ordinary, concrete things immediately around us we use these metaphors all the time, and on any larger, more puzzling subject we need constantly to try out new ones.

Strictly literal talk is in fact rather a rare and sophisticated activity, a late form of speech, hard to produce and useful only for certain limited purposes. It is not by any means the only language used in science. Scientists constantly use models and analogies drawn from outside their subject-matter, and they need to do this all the more vigorously where they are not doing 'normal science', but generating new ideas. Whole books have been written about Darwin's metaphors, and probably about Einstein's too.

Is all this symbolizing dangerous? Of course it is. Everything fertile and unpredictable is dangerous. Imaginative talk makes it impossible to disinfect thought by confining it in libraries for the use of licensed academics. Thought is incurably powerful and explosive stuff, not safely insulated from feeling and action, but integrally linked with both of them. *We think as whole people*, not as disembodied minds, not as computers. (That point is central to this book and will be developed especially in Chapter 3.) All ideas that are of the slightest interest to anybody can have unexpected emotional and practical consequences – consequences that cannot possibly be spelt out in advance. And, without this constant flow of ideas, life would grind to a halt.

Here, if you will believe me, is yet another thing that has made the imagery of water haunt me as suitable for philosophy. Useful and familiar though water is, it is not really tame stuff. It is life-giving and it is wild. Floods and storms have appalling force; seas can drown people, rivers carve out valleys. Then, too, rivers produce fertile plains and forests. Water works at the heart of life, and it works there by constant movement, continually responding to what goes on round it. Thought, too, ought to be conceived dynamically, as something that we do, and must constantly keep doing. The static model shown us by Descartes, of final proofs to be produced by science, proofs that will settle everything, is one more model that has very grave limitations.

So too, of course, is this talk of water. All analogies are imperfect, all of them have faults, all of them do only limited work. I am not suggesting that this one is any exception. I have tried to explain the work that it does do. But to be quite clear about it, we need to look (finally) at the question I raised in starting, the question about dignity.

DIGNITY AND DEPENDENCE

Is the approach I have been suggesting undignified? The reason why it can seem so is not, I think, just that it is too familiar and domestic, but that it postulates *needs*. It treats philosophy, like food and shelter, as something that we must have because we are in real trouble without it. We are perhaps more used to the thought that philosophy is splendid but gratuitous, and that it is splendid because it is gratuitous – something grand and exalted (like diamonds) which is not useful, but ought to be pursued all the same. On this view, intelligent people philosophize because they can see a special kind of supreme value in doing so, and perhaps everybody is capable of seeing this. But this taste is seen as something a bit removed from the rest of life, and independent of it. It is felt that our regard for philosophy ought to be a disinterested one, that there is something mean about dependence.

There really is a point in both these ways of talking, and it is not easy to balance them properly. The idea of disinterested detachment is indeed important. Pure knowledge, pure understanding, certainly is an end in itself, an aim which it is absurd to describe as 'useless'. (We will return to that topic in Chapter 5.) But this talk of disinterested detachment can be misleading, both in the case of knowledge and in that of art, because it can easily sound as if we were describing a luxury, a hobby, an extra. When Socrates said that the unexamined life is unliveable to man, I don't think he meant just that our species happens to have a peculiar taste for understanding, an unaccountable and noble impulse to philosophize.

That is the way people often do interpret this kind of claim, and it's particularly often brought forward as a reason for doing science. But Socrates was surely saying something much stronger. He was saying that there are limits to living in a mess. He was pointing out that we do live in a constant, and constantly increasing, conceptual mess, and that we need to do something about it. He knew that the presence of this mess, this chronic confusion, is something we don't much want to think about because it indicates the thoroughly undignified fact that we are inherently confused beings. We exist in continual conflict because our natural impulses don't form a clear, coherent system. And the cultures by which we try to make sense of those impulses often work very badly.

So – said Socrates – unless we acknowledge the resulting shameful confusions and do something to sort them out, none of our projects, whether grand or mundane, is likely to come to much. This means that we have to look at the confusions where the problems are actually arising, in real life. The kind of philosophy that tries to do this is now called Applied Philosophy. This suggests to some people that it is a mere by-product of the pure kind – a secondary spin-off from nobler, more abstract processes going on in ivory towers. But that is not the way in which European philosophy has so far developed.

Socrates started it by diving straight into the moral, political, religious and scientific problems arising in his day. He moved on towards abstraction, not for its own sake, but because it was needed in order to clear up the deeper confusions underlying these primary messes. The same is true of Kant's preoccupation with freedom, which shaped his whole metaphysic. Good metaphysics has always been directed by considerations which are practical as well as theoretical, substantial as well as formal. Metaphysicians who claim to be free from these considerations certainly haven't really got shot of them. They are merely unaware of their own motivations, which is no gain at all.

WHAT SHOULD WE DO?

Granted, then, that the confusions are there, is abstract philosophical speculation really a helpful remedy? Are the plumbers any use? Obviously this kind of speculation can't work alone; all sorts of other human functions and faculties are needed too. But once you have got an articulate culture, the explicit, verbal statement of the problems does seem to be needed.

Socrates lived, as we do, in a society that was highly articulate and self-conscious, indeed, strongly hooked on words. It may well be that other cultures, less committed to talk, find different routes to salvation, that they pursue a less word-bound form of wisdom. But wisdom itself matters everywhere, and everybody must start from where they are. I think it might well pay us to be less interested in what philosophy can do for our dignity, and more aware of the shocking malfunctions for which it is an essential remedy.

2

PRACTICAL UTOPIANISM

—— ·✦· ——

COMPREHENDING THE INCOMPREHENSIBLE

I HAVE been suggesting that thought and action, philosophy and life, are less alien, more closely connected, than we tend to suppose. How does this work out in politics? The main question here is rather a strange one. It is: how can we think effectively about dilemmas which are manifestly too big for us to handle?

We today aren't actually the first people who have faced this problem, though we often feel as if we were. The people who lived in earlier ages often found their world every bit as confusing and dangerous as we do. It may be true that our world actually is worse than theirs. But that made very little difference for the people involved. You can lose hope and drown just as well in seven feet of water as in seventy.

In the West, for instance, the future seemed utterly hopeless to many people during the break-up of the Roman Empire and again during the Thirty Years War. In many ways, too, things looked very black during the early years of the Industrial Revolution. The reformers who then set about the discouraging business of abolishing the slave trade, or attacking the state of factories in the 1840s, or rewriting political theory after the failed revolutions of 1848 (as Marx did), needed a remarkable degree of confidence to keep up their hope.

But people did do these apparently irrational things. And, though their contemporaries told them that it would be much more sensible to collapse into fatalistic inertia, most of us probably think now that they were right to neglect that advice.

This leads us back to my rather strange question. How is it psychologically possible for anyone to confront dilemmas which are – as those other dilemmas were to the people of their day – manifestly too big even to conceive of properly, let alone to handle? If we're to do anything at all in these situations, we need special ways of thinking. We have, as it were, to make our way through a desperately confused and dangerous landscape. We need light on the crucial features of that landscape, and we need good maps.

Those maps don't have to be fully detailed. In fact they must be limited and simplified, or we shan't make out the features that we need to see. Yet they do have to be detailed enough to make those features recognizable. They must be truthful enough to warn us about the difficulties, but not so alarming that we get utterly discouraged. All this is very hard, and it may sound as if these maps must be misleading. Yet they are not; they are just selective.

The people who have managed to retrieve desperate situations in the past have done so by somehow making maps of this kind. They have formed conceptual schemes, sets of ideas which somehow lit up the problems of the moment, problems that were proving impenetrable to traditional thinking. Those maps – those new conceptual schemes – must leave out, for the time, everything irrelevant, including endless further problems which can't be dealt with yet. They must bring forward the central issues, making them look clear and limited enough to tackle. They must also envisage distant possibilities which haven't yet been considered. Till that clarification is done, confusion reigns and people seem to face a gorgon which turns them to stone. They are paralysed by the mere tangle of conflicting considerations.

HANDY DEFENCES AGAINST THOUGHT

In these crises, people often conclude that the most practical thing is to stop thinking altogether. This, rather surprisingly, is a mistake. During drastic change, new ideas are not a luxury but a necessity. We need them, both as a tool for action and as a help to preserving our sanity – both in order to help us envisage our problems effectively and so as to avoid psychic disaster. But since it's very hard to produce these more suitable ideas, we often use instead other defence mechanisms which are much less satisfactory.

The simplest of these defences is, of course, just to forget about large-scale troubles altogether and we all do have to do this some of the time. But if we do it too much we may have to pay a heavy cost in psychic numbing and narrowing, even sometimes in actual depression and despair. Cutting ourselves off from the world blocks the springs of our life, because it shuts us off from reality. Even for our own inner health, we need sometimes to turn our minds to these monstrous topics.

You will notice that this is essentially a psychological discussion. It deals with our own responses, with the ways in which we can face these vast dilemmas or not face them, rather than directly with the dilemmas themselves. Of course this psychological problem is incomparably smaller than the outside dilemmas but it is still a weighty one because it concerns us so immediately. If we don't get started on it, we may find it hard to get any further. So it does seem to deserve some attention first.

CRUSADES AND JIHADS

To resume, then – our next simplest defence (after just avoiding these issues) is to polarize them into a black-and-white ritual combat between good and evil. The impulse to do this is very strong; we surely don't fully understand it. Tribal loyalty does, almost necessarily, form a part of our political efforts. But when we see other people disputing, we can usually see how much harm confrontation does. Yet it is surprisingly hard to apply that knowledge when we are involved ourselves.

If, however, we get disillusioned with the various available crusades, we may drop into an even odder polarization, abandoning thought altogether in favour of non-thought. We may become anti-intellectual Realists, rejecting all theory as simply irrelevant to practice. The whole mass of idealistic thoughts and intentions then looks like a gearwheel with no teeth, turning uselessly in the mechanism of the world. From that position, words like *Idealism* and *Utopianism* themselves become simply terms of abuse. Or, of course, we may go the other way and sign up as idealists who are too pure to dirty ourselves with action at all.

This game of Realist v. Idealist is paralysing because it divides the two sides of our own nature which need to work together for action. It divides these two sides even if (as can happen) it's combined with the crusading habit rather than replacing it. Thus, people who are officially conducting a crusade may still choose to play the role of victims, Idealists who are helpless because they are misunderstood by the Realists. They then naturally lose interest in the criticisms that might bring these sides together. In this mood we refuse to think about practical difficulties, so that we can't act or choose any positive policy for action. That can happen even to people who are officially clamouring for immediate change. It is, in fact, one of the commonest of the paralysing factors that waste the goodwill available for reform.

If, on the other hand, we choose to play as a Realist who knows the facts but is too clever to go in for ideals, we may know what the possibilities are all right but, since we have decided that the *status quo* can't be changed, we shall never find any reason to use this knowledge. (That, of course, is the Civil Servant's Syndrome.)

DIVISIONS OF LABOUR

It is surprising how hard it is to bring these two sides of our nature together. One very common way in which people do do it, is to take these roles in succession, starting life as an Idealist and moving to the Realist role as one gets older. This stereotype is immensely old. Or one can reverse it, acting in youth as a realistic rebel who has seen through the fuddy-duddy moral nonsense offered by one's parents.

This dramatic pattern is especially attractive in an age of rapid change. Plato displayed it shrewdly in the *Gorgias* where Socrates meets a sharp young politician named Callicles, an immoralist who gives a striking impression of having just read Nietzsche, Machiavelli and the latest postmodern treatments of ethics . . . [1] As it turns out, Callicles hasn't actually been reading anybody. As he explains, he radically despises all theoretical discussion. Thought and argument, he says, are occupations for boys, games to limber up little minds for the real world, amusements to be dropped when you get there. Adult life is a game too, but it's a violent and final one, a power game to be played as hard as possible for one's own hand. Anyone who lets himself be distracted from it by considerations of truth or consistency, let alone of other people's interests, is simply a fool.

Callicles, of course, is still with us today. In him, the division between Realist and Idealist, between thought and action, is unusually drastic. Callicles claims to throw ideals overboard entirely (though it is noticeable that he is often gripped by fantasies and indeed by conventions). Most people probably take a less extreme position than his, accepting that both aspects of life are necessary but dividing the labour. They commission one set of people to supply the ideals and another, different set to carry them out.

This drama can be played either between the generations or between the sexes. Women may be commissioned to have the ideals while the men do the real acting. Or, in a democracy, the voters may be supposed to have ideals and to shout their horror at current iniquities, thus forcing the administrators – who themselves have no views about morals – to make the practical changes. The politicians then form a sort of gear-mechanism, loosely connecting the two sides and linking the ideals with reality.

Up to a point these divisions of labour do work. But they are awkward, they waste a fearful amount of energy in friction and, as we know, there is something very uneasy about them. Two parties who see each other as (respectively) fools and knaves, humbugs and scoundrels, can't easily work in harmony together. This isn't a satisfactory principle for any division of labour.

IDEALS ARE NOT INERT

Ought we then perhaps to suspect that the game was wrongly set up in the first place? Is it possible that the two sides of our nature should not have got separated as they have? Perhaps, in fact, Realism and Idealism are *not* alternatives but two inseparable aspects of any true practical attitude. Our tendency to divide them is, however, remarkably strong. It is shown, rather comically, when people say (as they so often do) that some proposal is 'all right in theory but no good in practice'. A proposal that really *is* no good in practice has surely got something wrong with it in theory too. And a theory that doesn't fit the facts is a faulty theory. It needs changing.

This whole question is important to that rather large number of us today, including students, who spend our time doing intellectual work, some of us being actually paid to do it. Is our occupation with theoretical questions really just a self-contained humbug-factory, a web of idle dreams, fantasies and wish-fulfilments? Or are there also dreams which are not idle? *Are there effective dreams?*

On glancing round, it seems pretty plain that there are. The world is changing very fast, and certain dreams – some of them very bad dreams – evidently play a large part in directing that change. Some of those bad dreams formed the noxious part of Marxism. Another set of them has been active in the monstrous production of weaponry over the past century. Another – more noticeable at present – fuels the monetarist dream which promises us universal prosperity through 'trickle-down' from the uncontrolled working of the markets. These dreams have not just grown up spontaneously on their own, like weeds. They have all been deliberately produced by relatively recent thinking.

The seed of the monetarist project was sown by Social Darwinist dreamers in the last century. It arose, not just from factual beliefs current in their day, but also from a one-sided, unbalanced obsession with the ideal of freedom. This attachment was in its own way an idealistic vision and much of its strength has derived from that idealism. The trouble with it is simply that it *is* so one-sided. More generally, even the most cynical and disastrous doctrines usually do owe some of their strength to this kind of one-sided idealism.

Anyone, then, who habitually dismisses idealistic talk as mere idle vapouring, 'all right in theory but ineffective in practice', is not living in today's world. It is only in the most stagnant times that practices can be treated as fixed rocks on which the waves of theory will break without making any impression. Today, practices as well as theories fall constantly into the melting-pot.

Things, in fact, do change. And among the factors which change them, the accepted ideals of the day play a central part. The changing imaginative visions that figure in books, films and television programmes aren't just froth on the surface or pieces in a game. They have their effect; they can mean life or death, salvation or destruction. Yet the kind of reality that they have is strangely hard to grasp. Mostly, we oscillate between taking these ideas seriously and ignoring them as mere dreams or shadows.

When we see them as shadows, we easily drift into a kind of fatalism, into believing that the practical world is indeed immutable, armoured against anything we can think or do. That fatalism itself is, however, surely just one more rather ineffective emotional defence, a way of avoiding the notion that there still is something that we might do. It's a defence which splits off the practical from the reflective side of our nature, separating them as chemists separate substances that may explode if they get together. We leave these two parts of ourselves chronically at odds and let them take turns at influencing action. Thus, most of us respond sometimes to other people's cynical fatalism with idealistic protests and sometimes to other people's ideals with fatalistic ones.

DIALECTICAL TACTICS

Might all this opposition perhaps be just a useful dialectic, producing a synthesis in the end? Some philosophers have said so, but then, philosophers do tend to be argumentative people. They sometimes exaggerate the usefulness of conflict. Most often, debating only makes the gap between the disputants wider, which is why debating societies, especially for adults, have only a limited use. Each opponent tends to become more divided internally, practising the two roles separately without bringing them together. And when this internal debate is unacknowledged, there can't be any useful dialectic at all.

It is this inner division, not the outside difficulties, which can finally paralyse us, making us give up thought altogether. Even if the paralysis isn't complete, it can still poison our responses. The side that we officially oppose still gives trouble within us until it has been properly dealt with. There is then still cognitive dissonance – unresolved confusion in our thought and ambivalence in our feeling. This can badly distort the way in which we carry on controversies, making us violently unfair to our opponents, who stand for the rejected element. And it fixes the idea of a deep warfare between thought and feeling at the heart of our thinking.

THE UNSEEN CAMPAIGNERS

What are we to do about all this? I have been suggesting that the idea of thought as being impotent is just one more myth among others, a myth that we devise chiefly to defend ourselves against the exhausting business of confronting reality. This myth is remarkably selective. It draws a contrast between thought and action which lines up, in the oddest manner, with the division between virtue and vice. It suits the immoralist Callicles, who lurks in a corner inside most of us. The myth says that, while virtue is totally ineffective, iniquity actually *is* effective in the world, even though iniquity works through human consciousness just as much as virtue does.

There is, of course, a grim half-truth here – a half-truth so painful and so much suppressed that no wonder it looks like realism. A great deal of human behaviour is indeed so appalling that we try hard to forget about it. There is indeed a terrible lot of effective iniquity about. But when we have said this, realism calls on our bewildered imaginations to look further. The other half of this truth is the huge and quite effective effort that people are constantly making to fight against these iniquities and produce at least a drawn battle. As the Book of Ecclesiasticus puts it:

> Let us now praise famous men, and our fathers that begat us . . . All these were honoured in their generations, and were the glory of their times. But some there be which have no memorial, which are perished as though they had never been . . . And these were merciful men, whose righteousness hath not been forgotten. Their bodies are buried in peace, but their name liveth for evermore.[2]

We take all this effort for granted. But when those struggling people happen to relax their efforts, we quickly see how much worse things could easily be.

It is not just an idle cliché that 'things could be a lot worse'. It is a vital part of the truth. Human history, bad though it is, is still the product of constant conflict, a continuing struggle between the worse and the better. If you look at it from the devil's end (as C.S. Lewis does in *The Screwtape Letters*) you see that vice doesn't actually have things all its own way. The reason why we overlook this modest fact is, of course, our bitter disappointment that virtue hasn't achieved more than it has. This recognition is something that realism does demand of us. We are right to be disappointed, right, in a way, to be horrified, by the world. But our disappointment and horror don't license fatalism and resignation.

The balance is really difficult here. There is a fierce tension between ideals and reality, especially, of course, for people who are trying to do something to bridge the gap. This, too, is nothing new. Two thousand years ago Cicero, who was desperately attempting reform but depended on very corrupt allies, cried out that 'the trouble is that we have to work, not in Plato's *Republic* but in Romulus's pigsty'. When one is in that mood, it is natural to write off all expressions of ideals, including books like the *Republic*, as simply fantasies, dreams irrelevant to reality. But this very natural response surely misses the point. I would like to end by saying a word about the function of these books – these imaginary worlds, these so-called Utopias and dystopias. I think a glance at this topic may help us to see both why we need art as well as why we need philosophy. These books grow in an area where art and philosophy overlap.

THE ROLE OF UTOPIAS

In recent times, theorists have denounced Utopias and erected defences against attending seriously to them. This attack began during the Second World War, when several high-minded thinkers (notably Karl Popper and Richard Crossman) decided that Plato was a Fascist. Modern libertarians, however, have widened the charge in a way that accuses all such sweeping visions of narrowness and totalitarianism. Taken seriously, their objection damns William Morris and Ursula LeGuin as much as Plato. It applies, too, to the so-called dystopias – visions of evil like *Brave New World* and *Animal Farm* and *Player Piano* – because those visions too are propagandist and single-minded. They direct us as firmly from behind as the Utopias do from in front.

Robert Nozick, in his book *Anarchy, State and Utopia*, puts the libertarian accusation like this:

> Given the enormous complexity of man, his many desires, aspirations, impulses, talents, mistakes, loves, sillinesses, given the *thickness* of his intertwined and interrelated levels, facets, relationships ... and given the complexity of interpersonal institutions and relationships ... it is enormously unlikely that, even if there were one ideal pattern for society, it could be arrived at in this *a priori* fashion.[3]

Of course Nozick is right to warn us against seizing on a single one of these visions exclusively and forcing its pattern on society. But he means to do more than that. He wants to dissuade us from using any such vast and remote views of ideals at all. He calls on us to take up a standpoint which is wholly empirical, realistic and dream-free.

This is a quite impossible project. Every view of the world is selective and expresses some dream. Anyone who claims to show us only the complexity of the facts is a fraud. To return to the image we began with, any usable account must simplify the world. We have to represent large problems to ourselves on some kind of map, and we have to make these maps from some particular standpoint. That is the only way to get these matters within human comprehension.

Nozick himself is using such a selective map as much as anyone else. It's a map that is easily overlooked because it is so familiar. It is the Social Darwinist map, shaped by Herbert Spencer's travesty of evolutionary theory. It concentrates exclusively on one ideal – liberty, seen as a beneficent free-for-all leading infallibly to progress through the survival of the fittest.

In a way, this picture is itself just one more Utopia – one more vision of an ideal path for the human race. It looks more different than it is from the earlier ones because it is dynamic while they are static. Like Marxism, it concentrates much more on a series of means than on any eventual goal. But since both Spencerism and Marxism exalt and idealize the means they recommend quite as exclusively as other doctrines have exalted their goals, this difference is not necessarily very important.

HOW IMAGINATION WORKS

Let us look again at the way in which Utopias actually work. Two opposite sorts of charge have been brought against them. They are accused both of being unrealistically hopeful – of describing impossible reforms – and also of being totalitarian, describing over-organized places where no sensible person would want to live. But both charges seem to miss the nature of our imagination, the way in which it feeds on strange visions.

Writings like this aren't meant as literal blueprints for what ought to be built or as exact itineraries for our journey. Instead, they act as imaginative pictures of possible houses to be built or as searchlights, plunging their beams deep into the surrounding landscape at a single point to light up our journey. At times these searchlights show us distant mountains towards which we are travelling. These are landmarks which will serve to direct us even though we don't actually need to reach them, like signposts that say simply 'To the North'. At other times, they show us appalling precipices over which we might fall. They indicate possible long-term goals and dangers. They light up general directions. And they have to suggest these things in a way that is very far from literal, a way that must often be startling and paradoxical, because paradox can give our imagination the shock that it needs to start it working.

In this way, Utopias are no different from dystopias, though dystopias seem to work better today. Neither genre is realistic. The point is to make it possible for us to envisage a drastic general change, not just as a casual fantasy, but as really possible. This can be done equally by describing a much better world or by describing a worse one which would follow from certain existing trends, as dystopias do. Literal truth is beside the point in both cases, even though the incredible things proposed in Utopias do sometimes happen. For instance, Thomas More suggested a guaranteed nine-hour working day . . . [4] When these things do happen, they are naturally taken as matters of course. So they can then seem to lend force to the second objection, namely, that this is a thin and over-organized way of life.

But of course these books aren't holiday brochures, describing places where we would like to live. Like science fiction, they have to emphasize a few large-scale institutional points at the expense of detail. And because they have to take us to a world that is really far from where we now are they naturally tend to sound rather alarming. If this distant view is never seen – if a society simply never takes the trouble to notice how far it is from fulfilling its supposed ideals – then there is nothing to stop it becoming complacent about its present state.

Utopias then, like science fiction, can't afford to give life to their institutions by developing characters and humanizing the scene. They have to concentrate instead on some particular range of large changes, and they must exaggerate these so as to make them clear.

This does inevitably make them one-sided. So of course the critics are quite right to point out that we shouldn't take any one of these stories literally as a blueprint for reform. And since, in real life, this sort of one-sided simplification could only be imposed by force, attempts at it would be bound to lead to totalitarianism. That is why James Lovelock gets accused of ecofascism. And it has, of course, been the central trouble with Marxism.

PLURALISM IS NOT NIHILISM

But – and this is my central point – *we do still need these more distant, simplified visions.* If we try to work with a world-view which shows us only the complexity of existing facts, we lose our bearings and forget where we are going. And of course these supposedly realistic views aren't truly realistic either. Every account enshrines some particular ideals rather than others and expresses some dream. Our imagination needs, then, to be stimulated, not from one but from a hundred points on this spectrum. It needs to be stirred constantly from different angles by different aspects of the truth, if it is to keep its power of responding to what goes on.

Recently, certain 'postmodern' theorists have travestied this need for plurality of angles by recommending a mere lack of conviction, a kind of all-purpose 'irony' which is so sophisticated that it never commits itself to any position. This attitude is, of course, a relatively labour-saving response to the jubilant Social Darwinist free-for-all. It is a less exhausting option than the continuous fighting recommended by evolutionary prophets. All the same, it doesn't really make sense.

The reason why we have to be open to many kinds of message is not because none of them is ever true or false or – what comes to the same thing – because they are all equally so. Instead, it is because the whole truth is complicated and needs many of them. So far, Nozick and Mill are right. The world really is too complex to be explained by any single formula. That, however, does not make it sensible to talk as if all suggestions about it are equally valuable or valid. We cannot talk like this because we live here. We are not just detached spectators on another planet, writing doctoral theses about this one. We don't have the option of elegant, impartial scepticism. Although our information always is inadequate, we have to come off the fence and form opinions we can act on. We have to make choices.

That is where we need the full scope of our imagination, and it is where our imagination needs both art and philosophy. Most of art does not, of course, deal as directly with our practical dilemmas as Utopias and dystopias do. But all art embodies visions, and our visions express the ideals that move us. If we are to avoid collapsing in fatalistic resignation, we need constantly to drink at this spring. We need to find good visions because, if we don't, we will unavoidably be enslaved by bad ones. Good visions are the necessary nourishment of effective idealism.

3

HOMUNCULUS TROUBLE
—— ·◆· ——

Or, what is applied philosophy?

WHO IS SPEAKING, PLEASE?

PRACTICAL, POLITICAL thinking, then, is an activity that we cannot really avoid engaging in somehow. But how does it relate to our speculative thinking, if we try to do that too?

This raises the awkward question: inside the philosopher, who is it that does the philosophizing? I am sorry if this seems a confusing query. Life would certainly be simpler if we were so made that such questions couldn't arise. But politics, like everyday life, is full of choices to be made; and whenever we try to make a choice, a whole committee of little voices starts inside us, each urging us to a different decision. Any readers blest enough not to have frequent internal committee-meetings going on inside them will not see why we need to ask who's doing the thinking and will probably read no further. But most of us do understand it, I think, when we glance round at other professions.

Lawyers or doctors who hand over their business to a trained homunculus within – an automaton, a monomaniac clerk who seldom speaks to the rest of the personality, and who takes notice of nobody except the similar clerks inside other like-minded lawyers or doctors – such people often alarm us. Scholars who act on the same pattern can't, of course, usually do so much visible damage. But we are all familiar with the bad work that can result. And when that bad work is read by large numbers of students, the disaster that follows may not be negligible in terms of mere waste of life, even if the stuff were inert and not downright misleading – which it often is.

The difficulty is, of course, how to collect and use the great weight of skills and material that scholarship demands without compartmentalizing oneself to this disastrous extent. It is not a new problem. Plato portrayed some splendid learned monomaniacs who could pass without comment in any common-room today. But in our century, things are of course much harder because of the sheer mass of material. This has by now produced a degree of specialization that causes real alarm even in subjects where it is – up to a point – readily accepted because they live far from everyday life, such as physics. It is growing clear that beyond a certain point of fragmentation, the general direction of an enquiry cannot be intelligently controlled, nor can the information that is collected be properly understood and used.

PHILOSOPHERS IN A QUANDARY

What, however, about philosophy? Here the subject-matter is the maps or structures by which thought works, and – as would probably be agreed today – thought is not something quite separate from life. Yet, from the first beginnings among the Greeks, there have always been some parts of philosophy which were fiercely technical. Is it possible both to handle these properly and to do justice to the full richness of the questions as they arise in the life around us? Can anyone speak both as a fully instructed professional and as a whole human being?

It certainly is terribly hard. No doubt it does sometimes become necessary to make up one's mind which of these poles one is – in a crisis – most anxious to cling to. Yet in principle great efforts must be made to stick to both, and it is no less unprofessional to lose touch with one than with the other.

For a long time, the English-speaking philosophical tradition mostly nailed its colours defiantly to the pole of wholeness and life. Bacon, Hobbes, Locke, Berkeley, Hume and Mill all emphatically meant their writings to be widely read and to affect people's lives. Even Bertrand Russell still often did so. But William James and John Dewey were among the last influential figures to follow this track whole-heartedly. In the twentieth century, philosophy has largely gone with the rest of the academic world in accepting thorough specialization. I want to say that – right across that academic world – this move has been far too naive and whole-hogging. There has been much too little determination to combine the two ideals – to insist on still having ways of understanding the main map, even if one spends most of one's time digging in one corner of it. But in philosophy, and especially in moral philosophy, this need is surely obvious and vital.

In moral philosophy, indeed, it is now being widely felt and admitted. The desolating pointlessness of highly abstract 'meta-ethics', conducted between over-specialized homunculi, has brought its own nemesis. Talk about wider subjects has welled up all over the place and has ceased to shock the faculty, which is a good thing. Much, however, needs still to be done to sort out this enterprise; many bugs still need to be got out of the system. And one of these bugs infests the title under which these discussions are now authorized to happen. What is 'applied philosophy' and what is the 'pure philosophy' which is presumably needed to balance it?

SCIENCE, APPLIED AND PURE

It may be helpful here to start by looking at the distinction between pure and applied *science* – a distinction which has surely supplied the model for 'applied philosophy'. Peter Medawar, in a paper called 'Two Concepts of Science', complained that this distinction is not a very clear or sensible one. *All* good science (he said) involves a constant interplay between general principles and particular examples, between theory and observation, between contemplation and use, between thought and practice. *There are not two kinds of science*, radically divided according to the sources from which they are funded. The remotest speculations can easily turn out useful; the most practical enquiries can always throw up big theoretical issues.

There is (said Medawar) an important distinction here, but it is a different one. It is the distinction between general principles and particular cases, between the *a priori* and the empirical. This is a difference, but it certainly is not a gulf which allows them to be studied apart. And this important distinction (he goes on)

> is not the one we now make when we differentiate between the basic and applied sciences. The notion of *purity* has somehow been superimposed upon it, and in a new usage that connotes a conscious and inexplicably self-righteous disengagement from the pressures of necessity and use.

This distinction, he says, is not being made

> between the empirically founded sciences and those whose axioms were supposedly known *a priori*; rather it is between polite and rude learning, between the laudably useless and the vulgarly applied, the free and the intellectually compromised, the poetic and the mundane . . .

All this [he goes on] is terribly, terribly English . . . Making pure and applied science the basis of a class-distinction helps us to forget that it was our engineers and merchants who won for us that very grand position in the world from which we have now stepped down. It is not always easy to explain to foreigners the whole connotation of 'pure' in the context 'pure research' . . . [to explain the idea that] while pure science is a genteel and even creditable activity for scientists in universities, applied science, with all its horrid connotations of trade, has no place on the campus.[1]

Why – apart from mere original sin – have we come to think like this? Here Medawar makes an interesting parallel with the arts. In Britain, he observes, the art most loved and honoured is poetry. 'Hereabouts, a man inspired is typically a poet inspired'. But, 'unfortunately, there is no such thing as Applied Poetry, or rather there is, but we think little of it.' Commissioned poems, ordered from Poet Laureates or from tombstone-makers and valentine-smiths, don't rank high in public estimation. Elsewhere things are different, since

in countries in which poetry is not the top art-form, the idea of *occasional* or *commissioned* art is commonplace and honourable, and there is correspondingly less fuss, if any, about the distinction between pure science and applied. Tapestry and statuary, stained glass, murals and portraiture . . . fire music, water music and funeral marches, all are commissioned, and the act of being commissioned can light up the imagination.

ROMANTICISM, SNOBBERY AND CREATIVITY

On this diagnosis, contempt for commissioned work and exclusive exaltation of what is spontaneous are aspects of the Romantic creed. They are part of the attempt to exalt individual genius by detaching it from society. And though this is valuable both for science and for the arts, by encouraging original thought, it is quite wrong to exaggerate it into a dismissal of the communal efforts in which that thought eventually finds expression. On the poetic side, insistence on the lonely genius of Blake or Baudelaire can make us forget that Shakespeare and Aeschylus were successful working playwrights.

And in science, while it is right to stress the need for solitary wonder and musing – and indeed that stress is very much needed today – it is quite wrong to suppose that people can only muse creatively in conditions where the results are sure to be useless. Mendel is not disqualified from being a great and original scientist because he started his enquiries in order to help the local farmers, nor is Pasteur so disqualified because his greatest work was done in response, first to difficulties about fermentation in brewing, and then to medical problems.

Medawar is saying two things. First, that the distinction of pure v. applied science is a mess. It jumbles together at least three quite different distinctions. Second, that it is also pernicious. It adds to this brew a bogus evaluative element of snobbish contempt for the part that is 'applied'. Science (he protests) does not come in two kinds, first- and second-class. Instead there are many sciences, and the three genuine divisions mentioned criss-cross them all in quite different ways.

I think that he is right, and that on the whole the same thing is true for philosophy. But before coming to that, there is yet a fourth distinction to be added to the three already mentioned. We already have antitheses

1 between particular cases and general principles,
2 between what turns out actually useful and the actually useless, and
3 between what is commissioned and what is spontaneous.

ON THE BEAUTY OF NOT KNOWING THINGS

When we turn to the Oxford English Dictionary, however, we find yet a fourth canon. Under 'pure' we read:

> Of a study or practice; restricted to that which essentially belongs to it; not including the relations with kindred or connected subjects. Often denoting the simply theoretical part of a subject, apart from its practical application, as in 'pure mathematics'.

Now since the word 'pure' has an evaluative meaning, which is usually favourable, this raises some questions, more especially when we read one of the examples given (dated 1903): 'He is a pure physicist; he does not know chemistry'.

Is there anything especially good about *not* knowing other subjects than one's own, or about *not* knowing the relations between one's own subject and kindred or connected ones? The idea that there is implies that all outlying knowledge is only a distraction from a certain set of central and dominant truths which are the essence of the subject. That would imply that the 'subjects' named are natural units, perfectly divided. They must each be so separate, so fully formed, that there can be no question about what is essential to them.

This is surely an odd story. The history of learning shows how, again and again over time, the whole conception of what a particular study is, and of what is essential to it, can need to be modified, and this often happens in response to challenges from a different field. An obvious example is the invasion, first of geology, then of biology, by historical methods during the late eighteenth and early nineteenth centuries, eventually producing the study of evolution. Biologists like Richard Owen who supported the earlier, unhistorical way of thinking bitterly resisted this stain on the purity of their study, but in vain.

And again, the list of available studies has not been given to us once for all in the tablets of the law. New ones constantly emerge. To allow them to do so, important work always has to be done on and outside the borders of several existing studies. Moreover, the main subjects themselves often split, and sometimes even die, leaving their remaining assets to be divided among several heirs. The map of academic subjects is not a lot more permanent and God-given than the political map of Europe. Poland and Estonia come and go; Austria contracts, Czechoslovakia and Yugoslavia appear and are lost again . . . How, then, could this idea of academic purity ever have gained such influence?

The answer surely lies in the example cited by the dictionary, the case of mathematics. Here indeed is a study which does have fairly definite boundaries. Here too is one that functions in two tolerably distinct ways. Its simplest stages are used for practical purposes by all sorts of people, while its more complex developments are esoteric, highly technical and are, as far as most of us can see, well isolated from the rest of life. Much the same thing is true of logic. These two timeless and formal non-empirical branches of thought have surely supplied the chief model for the pure/applied distinction. This is not surprising, because from Plato's time on, a string of great philosophers have especially admired these abstract studies and have held them up as a pattern for all other enquiries. But how many other branches of thought are at all like them in this matter?

DEPT. OF APPLIED HISTORY

An interesting example might be the idea of pure and applied history. Could there actually be a sub-set of historians who specialized in merely applying the truths which others established? This would be odd, and for obvious reasons. When we apply the findings of history to present-day affairs – when we see parallels, and wonder how to work them out in detail – we need to get those findings right. We need not just reliable data, but also good thinking, the kind of conceptual grasp which brings the data together in a way that has important implications. And this kind of thinking – this interpretation of the data – is itself an essential part of all historical work.

History as written is never just data, because such pure data simply would not be intelligible. They have to be selected and recombined. In spite of all possible efforts of objectivity, there can be no such thing as neutral history. Therefore, though historical interpretation is, at a basic level, something that all of us can do, its higher and more serious reaches are part of the work of those who establish the findings in the first place. They are not something that could be left to a separate tribe of humble appliers.

Do academic historians sit in an ivory tower doing pure speculation, and then handing out their results to an inferior application-expert, who touches his forelock, accepts them uncritically, goes off and applies them? No, but then, that is not the relation between physicist and engineer either. The metaphor which the word 'applied' so easily suggests, of intellectual plans ready-made by thinkers and then carried out by non-thinkers, is unworkable. If, therefore, a serious historian were to be asked whether there is a division between pure and applied history, the answer might surely be quite near to the one which Medawar gives about science. 'There are not two things called pure and applied history. History is one study. It is one because the past is one, an immense, continuous field for enquiry covering many areas and using many methods. All its enquiries can be pursued from different motives and used for different purposes, both practical and speculative. Of course, too, this work can be funded in various ways, but the source of funding does not – or at least it certainly should not – change the nature of the subject.'

PURITY PUZZLES

What, then, about applied philosophy? Here too, it seems to me, some kind of class-distinction is felt to operate, and I want to pin down the ideas that lie behind it. They are perhaps quite close to those that distort the case of science, centring on the same misconceived fable about the time-order. The pattern suggested is that first A does the real philosophy, then B applies it. Thus the serious work

– the hard and original thinking – would always be done by the pure theorists; the appliers would be beta-people who accepted their results, perhaps worked them out in minor details if that were necessary, and put them into effect. This impression is not removed but becomes even stronger if we replace the word *pure* by words like *basic* or *fundamental*, as is often done in the case of science.

WHERE QUESTIONS ARISE

This is the Band-Aid model of applied philosophy, by which highly abstract 'moral theories', devised by homunculi working in seclusion, have only to be directly applied to the world. R.G. Collingwood proposed a far more realistic story, which starts much further back, by asking how philosophical problems *arise* in the first place. They arise (said Collingwood) not just between homunculi or in universities but in whole cultures, out of clashes and conflicts between the presuppositions that are currently in use. These are also clashes between the large conceptual schemes by which everybody lives, because those schemes are built on these presuppositions, which are therefore directly expressed in people's lives – including, of course, in literature and the other arts.

Philosophical work starts, then, with the task of listening, of understanding these clashes and conflicts, and it continues through prolonged and difficult efforts to articulate them better. Examples would be the cluster of conflicts that arose in ancient Greece between the ideas of Nature and Custom, and the still larger mass of clashes that have surfaced, in the last three centuries, between the various ways of thinking that collide around the notion of freedom – including various forms of the mind–body problem.[2]

Collingwood said that this work of articulating conflicts was historical as well as philosophical because, as he rightly pointed out, it calls in the first place for careful observation and description of the existing confusions. We have to understand how people are actually thinking if we want to know where their thought is going wrong; and in order to understand how they are thinking, we often vitally need to grasp how they are living too. This essential historical slant needs, however, to be balanced by an emphasis on the non-historical work that must be done if we want, not just to identify these confusions, but also to clear them up. How do we make the conceptual changes that are needed?

Collingwood's work was incomplete here, because he became so devoted to the historical model that he often wrote as though merely describing the confusions would be enough to remove them. This idea was probably made more plausible by the early, optimistic model of psycho-analysis in which 'A trouble shared is a trouble got out of the system' – a bit like unblocking the plumbing – a model which was widely accepted in his day.

If there really were no possibility of working to cure confusions by suggesting new and positive ideas, our job would just be to record fatalistically what is wrong, like bus-passengers who cannot influence the driver but who still want the truth about their journey to be known. Though Collingwood did not manage to explain clearly what the practical, constructive role of philosophy ought to be here, he did not accept this passive, back-seat or ivory-tower role for it either. He was convinced that it ought to be active. But how?

WHAT WE APPLY IS PHILOSOPHY

What is needed, surely, is recognition that anyone who successfully articulates existing confusions is always restating them in a way that suggests a particular way to cure them. Thus thinkers like Rousseau, Kant, Mill and Nietzsche, in drawing attention to current confusions about the notion of freedom, were constantly reshaping the concepts used for these topics. They did not do this just in the interests of clarity. That interest would often be best served by dropping an awkward topic altogether. They did it in order to take a particular moral stand. Along with the confusions of the day, they articulated their own positive counsel about better ways in which people ought, not only to think, but also to live.

Large confusions have to be sorted out in life as well as in thought. In 'applying philosophy' to the world, what we are doing is using conceptual skills, in which we can to some extent be trained, on problems which are not yet shaped and processed to yield to them easily. The picture is *not* one of applying a Band-Aid to a standard cut, but of applying our minds to new and difficult matters. This is what those who have given the word philosophy its current meaning have been doing. Kant's or Mill's metaphysic is a metaphysic of morals as well as of science and, in building it, both of them gave much serious philosophical attention to questions of what ought to be done about the detailed, practical problems of their day. (It is particularly strange that Utilitarianism, whose founding fathers were above all practical reformers, should now so often be viewed as primarily a piece of theoretical academic dogma.)

This practical commitment of the great metaphysicians is of course often obscured for us now by our habit of attending almost exclusively to what are certified to be the greatest and most central books by each author. Thus, as Collingwood pointed out, the life of Oxford philosophers was much eased by the happy discovery that each great thinker had enshrined his whole thought in a single volume, by good luck, usually one printed in Everyman's Library . . . If one breaks out to study their works more widely, nearly all the great philosophers turn out, not only to have had much wider and more specific interests, but to have been deeply influenced by them in forming their central ideas.

IS IT TOO SPECIFIC?

Some professional philosophers today, if confronted with one of these 'minor works' that the mighty dead have indiscreetly produced, are inclined to growl that it is 'not really philosophy' or, still more oddly, 'nothing to do with philosophy'. I have often received this answer when I have cited things like Plato's discussions of the different kinds of love, especially Aristophanes' speech in the *Symposium* and the other myths, or of course anything by Nietzsche, or even Mill *On the Subjection of Women* – a topic to which we will return in Chapter 6. In this last case however, the more usual response is a slightly irritated one, as though the example were obviously unfair. 'Oh well – *political* philosophy . . .', they say, rather in the tone of someone who has been taken into the garden to admire the flowers, and then finds that they are plastic. Political philosophy can't actually be proved not to be an examinable part of the subject, but it still isn't supposed to be real philosophy.

Why on earth not? Here are conceptual problems of the first importance, being dealt with by essentially philosophical methods – that is, by boldly outlining current confusions, and suggesting ways in which both the concepts and the parts of life where they are used could be better handled. At the respectable end, I think the objection often felt is the first one that Medawar mentioned – namely, a sense that these topics are too specific. Trained philosophers today still tend to feel that there could be no good reason for Plato to talk especially about *love*. He should have seen that the topic could be adequately covered by a general discussion of the nature of emotion, or perhaps of 'personal relations'. Similarly, while the rights of individuals are admitted to be a suitably general topic for ethical discussion, the differences between the situations of men and women are not.

The mistake here does not lie in thinking that general principles are very important. They are. It lies in supposing that you can properly decide *which* general principles to talk about without having first intelligently examined the range of cases where trouble is building up. When we don't do this, our generalizations tend to get further and further removed from reality, because they are tacitly referring to a fixed range of examples, inherited from theorists facing different problems. And that range of examples itself tends to get narrower and narrower if new ones are not constantly being given.

THE ONE AND THE MANY

This narrowing, to my mind, has long been happening over questions about the meaning of social relations. As plenty of people have pointed out, prolonged insistence on Enlightenment doctrines of social atomism – on the utter separateness of each individual – has systematically distorted, not just the way we think but the way we live. Egoistic individualism isn't what we need more of. But our philosophical language still tends to imprison us in it.

Social atomism was of course needed in the first place for political reasons. The optional social contract has been, and still is, a useful model for many large-scale institutions. But in many smaller contexts it is not much use, and there are places, especially in personal life, where it is pernicious. In our present crowded, fluid, mobile way of life, loneliness is becoming a serious and threatening problem. Psychiatrists and therapists report a continuing shift from more sociable neuroses to solitary ones, made terrible by the patient's inability to communicate about them at all. In such a world, we surely need fresh thinking about the sense in which we are *not* hard, discrete, billiard-ball-like atoms, but are organically related, members one of another. We need to sort out helpful from unhelpful ways of expressing that fact.

As it happens, earlier philosophers often don't give us too much help here, because many of them were themselves engaged in the great individualistic enterprise, which was in its day indeed valuable. Plato was one of the exceptions. He did try to understand something of what individual human beings can mean to each other, and he did know that total independence of other people was not the whole of virtue. So did Aristotle and Butler, so did Martin Buber.

I am not sure whether I have missed some new development here, but I would be glad to know what philosophers are now developing this point[3]. Simple individualism seems often still to be taken for granted as the obvious, main moral truth, not just in notable places like Rawlsian political theory, but on topics which are not thought of as being moral or political at all, like personal identity. It seems strange to discuss this topic without direct, detailed attention to the many important and varied ways in which, in daily life, we can often feel ourselves *not* to be just one person, but identified in one way or another with others.

'REAL' PHILOSOPHY

If pregnancy and identification with one's child are topics too difficult for some people to handle, couldn't we at least hear something about simple cases of co-operation, like playing in an orchestra? There is also (as I mentioned at the start of this chapter) an important range of cases of inner dialogue and conflict, cases where each of us seems to be *more* than one person. And both these kinds of experience are often of enormous significance in our lives. What is it that makes philosophers discussing personal identity ignore these issues and focus their attention almost entirely on highly schematic, imaginary examples drawn from science fiction?

This is only one of the very odd omissions that can be perpetuated by the habit of highly abstract, conventional discussion, into which our homunculi will always lead us if we don't discipline them. They can do excellent work for us, but they always need to be supervised with the utmost sharpness to make sure that they don't take over things that they don't understand. Where they are not controlled, the most fascinating topics can get ignored. Thus, two excellent pieces of contemporary 'applied philosophy' – Sissela Bok's book *Lying* and Peter Singer's *Animal Liberation* – both treat subjects of obvious interest which were almost completely neglected by other philosophers at the time when they wrote.[4] By pulling those topics into the area of discussion, these authors have not just done us a practical service, but have also drawn attention to larger and more general philosophical issues which had been neglected along with this range of cases. The same thing is still more obviously true of Mill's *On the Subjection of Women*.

One reason why people object to specificity may perhaps be the fact that there has long existed a certain amount of rather bad moral philosophy, written about certain specific public topics, notably euthanasia and abortion. The trouble with this work was not that it was too specific, but that it was bad. There is no reason why philosophy with a direct application to specific areas of life should be bad and in fact a great deal of it has been very good. Nor is there any reason why the topics emerging should only be – as these were – ethical ones, or ones on the borders of ethics and politics. All kinds of big philosophical issues can and do emerge, just as Medawar pointed out that big scientific issues can emerge from scientific work undertaken for practical reasons.

This fertility has, however, been largely concealed from recent generations of philosophy students either by ignoring current affairs altogether, or by treating them in a way that carefully plays down that relevance. This tendency is, I think, dying, and the sooner it dies the better. When it has died – when a much wider range of material is accepted as obviously calling for 'real philosophy' – the need for a separate category of 'applied philosophy' may well vanish. Until this has happened, that awkward phrase will probably have to be used as a slogan, a lever to bring about a bit of affirmative action ('We need more Applied Philosophy . . .'). But it still isn't a clear name, and we need to keep an eye on its dangers. It easily suggests that there really should be a separate caste of homunculi doing the real philosophical work before the people who have to use the morality can be trusted to start thinking about it. And that is a mistake.

4

MYTHS OF INTELLECTUAL ISOLATION

—— •❖• ——

THE KNOWLEDGE MINES

SOCIAL ATOMISM has recently had some rather remarkable effects in education. We might ask, for instance, what kind of assumptions about the acquiring of knowledge could make it seem plausible that research is a quite separate activity from teaching and always outranks it? That idea is embodied now in current official educational policy. Yet it surely contradicts the common experience of educators, who have generally agreed that *docendo discimus*: by teaching, we learn.[1] There is, however, at present one quite prevalent way of thinking which might lead people to embrace this new policy. It is the approach which treats information, not as a forest through which we are already struggling, and which we chiefly need to map more clearly, but as a rare and precious metal, ingots of which must be brought from afar. These ingots are supposedly hard to fetch from their distant source. But, once fetched, they are not hard to handle, since they are shaped to fit slots in the heads of those who will finally have to use them. Teaching simply consists of dropping each ingot into its destined slot.

This model is not often openly defended. It is usually mentioned only to point out its faults. Yet it seems to be quite influential in practice. It works, for instance, in many scientific institutions where distinguished academics regularly delegate teaching work to their subordinates. Other scholars too often do this with first-year teaching, which is the stage when students commonly form their main conception of their subject. Again, on a University Promotions Committee I have seen colleagues recoil in astonishment at praise of a candidate's teaching, much as if somebody had suddenly said 'He cooks so well' or 'She grows lovely roses'.

Now the ingot model, in itself, would not be of much philosophical interest. But it is only a crude, extreme example of a whole set

41

of bad patterns on which learning, and more generally the whole way in which ideas develop, is currently conceived. These models isolate the learner, so that thought is seen as developing entirely inside a single brain. The ingot model is surprisingly close here to the herbaceous one which has had so wide an influence in early education. Rousseau's benign gardener is certainly a much more sympathetic operator than the ingot-placer, and differs from him in insisting that the child has, and must develop, its own active potentialities. But both place their pupils in a social vacuum, where no fraternal communication is needed for learning.

Rousseau establishes the notorious total isolation of his pupil from other children at once on the opening page of *Émile, or Of Education*:

> Tender, anxious mother, I appeal to you. You can remove this young tree from the highway and shield it from the crushing force of social conventions . . . From the outset raise a wall round your child's soul; another may sketch the plan; you alone should carry it into execution.

In the sequel, it is of course not the mother who fills this alarming role. The parental function, which might involve untidy entanglements with other background figures, is quietly handed to the solitary tutor, a figure who is a pure representative of abstract theory, uncorrupted by any specific social context.

The points of philosophic interest which this matter raises are now, I hope, in sight. This isolation of the individual is seriously distorting, not just for educational purposes, but for wider moral and political ones, and it bears on our whole conception of personal identity. The kind of abstract intellectual being, who needs a social contract to show him whether he should choose to belong to the human race, has been a useful fiction for many practical purposes, but we are by now reaching the limits of his usefulness and becoming a good deal inconvenienced by his faults. John Rawls has well exploited his remaining virtues. Many things that make him an unsuitable model for our thought have already been listed. But I do not know that his strange way of learning has been especially noted.

POPPER'S SCIENTIFIC METHOD

Why should philosophers note it? Well, one reason might be that most people engaged in philosophy are actually teaching or learning it, or doing both. An unrealistic, over-isolating view of these enterprises

42

could obviously distort this work. But the point is equally important for people outside academia. This kind of isolating approach misdescribes, not just children's learning, but that of adults as well. For instance, here are some famous words of Karl Popper's which are well-known as a prescription for scientific method, but which seem equally remarkable for their social implications. At a glance, Popper might seem to be conceding that scientists are not usually solitaries, for he uses the pronoun 'we'. But he leaves no doubt that 'we' simply means 'each one of us'.

'We' start, says Popper, with only a vague idea of our problem:

How, then, can we produce an adequate solution? Obviously, we cannot. We must first get better acquainted with the problem. But how?
My answer is very simple; by producing an inadequate solution and by *criticizing it* . . . In this way, we become acquainted with the problem, and may proceed from bad solutions to better ones – provided always that we have the creative ability to produce new guesses, and more new guesses.

He explains that we do this repeatedly, until finally

we begin to see the ramifications of the problem, its sub-problems and its connection with other problems. (*It is only at this stage that a new conjectured solution should be submitted to the criticism of others, and perhaps even published*) . . . At the next step our tentative solution is discussed; *everybody tries to find a flaw in it and to refute it* . . . [producing] a competitive struggle which eliminates those hypotheses which are unfit . . . From the amoeba to Einstein, the growth of knowledge is always the same; we try to solve our problems, and to obtain, *by a process of elimination*, something approaching adequacy in our tentative solutions.[2]

The emphases are mine. What kind of a world is this, where each hypothesis springs fully-formed from the brain of a single inventor, who mentions it to nobody until the time of its publication, after which the first contribution that anyone else makes is to attack it?

As we know, this is not really the way in which infant ideas get reared. From their first germination, they normally grow in public, in the common soil of the community. They occur to somebody, who mentions them, and they begin to be talked about. Their growth becomes possible because of shifts in the general climate of thought, and is fostered by half-conscious contributions from many sources for a long time before any one person thinks them out explicitly. When that does happen, these ideas are still not withdrawn from general circulation under some sort of copyright or Official Secrets Act by their first sponsor. People who get interested in them usually want to share them with others, and that fertile sharing is the main source of their further development. Of course elimination plays its part in discriminating among various emerging possibilities. But the main work of developing them is the positive, constructive, imaginative process of building them and thinking out better ways to use them, and this work is normally best carried on co-operatively, among circles of friends and acquaintances.

I am not, of course, denying that outsiders can sometimes spoil a promising piece of thinking, if it is exposed to them too early. Of course, too, ideas do also sometimes draw great advantage from phases of intense private concentration by a single person. These phases are indeed necessary for their full development. But the kind of biographical interest that we now take in occasional recorded cases of such concentration blinds us to the equally necessary, wide background of contribution from others. (For instance, Descartes' justly celebrated story of his solitary meditations so stirs us that we forget even what he himself says of his early debt to this teachers and friends.) Countless, equally valuable, similar periods of concentration by other people, which go quite unrecorded, and many seminal interchanges between them, are needed as well. Our mistake does not lie exactly in exaggerating the originality of the few inventors that we have heard of, for it is great, but in misrepresenting the kind of thing that it is, and in absurdly undervaluing what others have done to make it possible. 'Creativity' is unrealistically thought of as a private process of generation *ex nihilo*.

IDEAS ARE FOR SHOOTING DOWN

This story of Popper's has of course been well criticized from a number of other angles besides the social one that I am stressing now. By isolating his individual scientists from one another, Popper has notoriously also isolated their hypotheses, both from each other and from the whole background of thought that made their production possible. Instead of working together to improve their existing ideas, his imagined scientists, each in his own cell, creatively produce out of nowhere streams of quite new, disconnected 'guesses' which they toss in the air like clay pigeons and most of which are then shot down. It has by now been made plain that this is not the way in which thought actually develops, though that news has unfortunately not yet got through to all the scientists. *But nobody would ever have thought of suggesting or accepting this bad picture if they had not first been gripped by the equally unreal model of pervasive interpersonal competition.*

The distorted intellectual model of competition between individual ideas arises from the still more distorted social model of competition as the basic mode of intellectual interaction between individual people. This model does not (of course) really have any interesting connexion with biology. Its Darwinian varnish is just a modish dress for simple, old-fashioned controversial pugnacity. The fact that a hypothesis 'survives' in controversy has no fixed bearing on its chances of being right. Nor does the sharpness of controversy reliably tend to favour the emergence of good hypotheses – in fact, it often hinders it. Controversial sharpness and mildness are in themselves quite neutral qualities. What matters is whether the disputants know which things to be sharp or mild about.

Popper's model does of course rightly recommend impartiality, but it is the impartiality of general destruction. Instead of saying, 'try to cherish other people's children as you would your own' it says, 'shoot your own children as readily as you would other people's'. The reason why this strange advice has been welcomed is that it is indeed slightly better than the simple, unreconstructed military model of controversy, where no-one even tries to be impartial at all. If we ask why, at this time of day, people should still need to be told that this crude military model is bad, we find a situation rather like that over the ingot model of learning. Both these models are so powerfully seductive that, while it is easy to talk about abandoning them, it is immensely hard to do it.

MY ARGUMENTS ARE BIGGER THAN YOURS

Plato exposed the disastrous faults of the military approach long ago in his *Euthydemus*, where a couple of retired boxers who undertake to win every argument by their 'eristic' skills, were exhibited to discredit it. Plato, one of the few philosophers who has treated the interpersonal workings of thought seriously as an important aspect of philosophy,[3] found it easy to discredit the cruder effects of this approach. Yet he by no means showed a way to get clear of it. Even in the *Euthydemus*, the pugilists' unscrupulous tricks often bear a disquieting resemblance to some of Socrates's own favourite methods.[4]

And if we look at later scholarly controversy, it is surely clear that the military model still exerts enormous power. Our talk of attacking and defending positions, of flank attacks and last bastions and surprise assaults, is not just a dead metaphor. A much greater proportion of the articles in the journals is primarily destructive – intended to attack someone else's position – than is primarily constructive, intended to say something new.

Many people, indeed, would defend this disproportion as a fertile dialectic. Even scholars who are not themselves especially argumentative tend to accept, with Popper, that sharp disagreements produce an especially healthy climate for encouraging thought. Does our experience actually confirm this? I suspect that people who take this line do not notice that they are taking for granted the positive, co-operative, constructive phase of the development – as Popper himself surely does – and mentioning only the secondary phase of destructive criticism. But constructive co-operation cannot safely be taken for granted. The lop-sided public image affects practice. People forget how much we need to work together. Graduate students are left in solitude, each to fetch his own ingot of information, or to generate creatively his own parthenogenetic succession of hypotheses. (I deliberately say 'his' because this traditional model is essentially a male one. Everybody concedes, however uneasily, that female creativity does not work quite like this.) Different specialities see less and less of each other. Research becomes separated from teaching precisely because these crude models simply provide no language for expressing the vital need for interaction between thinkers at all levels – for a rich, varied and cohesive community within which ideas can get the varied nourishment they need.

Again, it must be plainly said that controversial sharpness has in itself no particular value. Most things that anybody says contain some parts that are wrong and some that are right. There is nothing intrinsically better about always preferring to concentrate on the faulty ones. Welcoming and developing somebody else's view is in general at least as likely to be valuable as attacking it. The notion that opposition is, as such, healthier is an expression of competitive individualism, an ideology which here goes beyond distorting our moral and political thinking, and corrupts our notion of what reasoning is. Individualism paints reasoning as consisting essentially of separate 'arguments', conceived as clashes between distinct opinions, owned in principle by distinct people, each of whom should aim to vanquish the other. The disputants are related like boxers or duellists or, at best, more discreetly, like rival litigants. But the law-court, if it is a law-court, is defective. There is here no judge or jury commissioned to comprehend the whole dispute and bring it to a rational conclusion. Both sides are simply there to win.

What other models ought we to use instead? I have repeatedly suggested the parallel with exploring an unknown piece of country, something which is much better done co-operatively than in competition. Or again, how about considering thought ecologically, as a country to be lived in and cultivated, so that the problem is: which life-forms to encourage and which to control? This is very much the pattern that Aristotle suggested by talking about 'saving the phenomena', by which he meant looking first at the existing forms of thought to see what can be made of them before launching something quite new. You don't start your ecological work with a flame-thrower. The practice of many other good philosophers has conformed to this pattern. But I do not know whether anybody has explicitly set it out as a model.

ENTER WITTGENSTEIN

The trouble with the military, duelling and forensic models is that they force people to contract their own views within a defensible area. This lays down a division of labour by which big questions are always somebody else's business. The legitimate and necessary process of outlining a particular topic for philosophical discussion is extended here into a systematic avoidance of large difficulties. In a drastic passage that has surely supplied the model for much avoidance of this kind, little though he would have liked such an interpretation, the young Wittgenstein wrote in the *Tractatus*:

> The correct method in philosophy would really be the following: to say nothing except what can be said, i.e., propositions of natural science ... and then, whenever *someone else* wanted to say something metaphysical, to demonstrate to him that *he* had failed to give a meaning to certain signs in his propositions. Although it would not be satisfying to *the other person* – he would not have the feeling that we were *teaching him philosophy* – this method would be the only strictly correct one.[5] [Emphases mine]

Here, all the difficulties are suddenly located inside 'the other person' – namely, a pupil – instead of within the author's own thought. Wittgenstein gives a strange, abrupt priority here to the job of converting 'the other person' over the internal task of making the doctrine itself fully plain. It is by no means clear, for instance, whether he means the category of 'natural science' to include such things as history and everyday observation, or whether these are meant to fall inside 'metaphysics'. The philosophical legislator surely needed to sort such points out before starting to teach them to others.

When he wrote this passage, Wittgenstein was indeed convinced that his *Tractatus* doctrine *was* perfectly clear and final. But since he also thought that hardly anybody else would be able to understand it,[6] he clearly felt the need for some way of overcoming other people's emotional resistance to considering it at all.

This is a predicament in which people with new and surprising ideas do often find themselves. But it has to be dealt with in legitimate and respectful ways. Plato gave great attention to this difficulty, devising his myths in order to help conversion, to show his general meaning in imaginative form. He separated them carefully from the argument proper, recognizing that such imaginative devices, though relevant, are not authoritative, and must not be used to extract uncomprehending submission. But silencing someone in the way that Wittgenstein recommends is just as much an imaginative device as a myth is. It works by attacking *the other's* confidence. This can quite legitimately be done as a momentary move when one wants to take the enquiry in a new direction. It can then really be necessary to say 'you're asking the wrong question'. But this move has to be followed by explaining what would be the right question. When it is used instead as a power-ploy, a territory-marker to protect philosophers from hard questions, it is illicit.

KNIFE-GRINDERS TO THE INTELLIGENTSIA

That, however, is how it often has been used. Thus, in the emotivist manifesto marking out the territory of moral philosophy at the outset of *Ethics and Language*, C.L. Stevenson wrote:

The purpose of an analytic or methodological study, whether of science or ethics, is always indirect. It hopes to send *others* to their tasks with clearer heads and less wasteful habits of investigation. This necessitates a continual scrutiny of what *those others* are doing . . . but it does not require the analyst, as such, to participate in the enquiry that he analyses. In ethics, any direct participation of this sort might have its *dangers*; it might deprive the analysis of its detachment and distort a relatively neutral study into a plea for some special code of morals . . . The present volume has the limited task of *sharpening the tools which others employ.*[7]

Now criticizing moral concepts is indeed a distinct job from using them, but why should it be a job allotted to a different set of people? This strange division of labour leaves 'the others' – the ones who actually have the moral problems – to deal with them without philosophical help, while the detached philosophers stick to the supposedly value-free job of finding certain basic forms which are common to all of them. They will evidently do this best if they themselves have no moral views at all, since this indifference will best guarantee their detachment. If we applied this same method to science (as Stevenson suggests) it would seem to follow that philosophers should not commit themselves to any particular opinion such as (for instance) the Copernican or Darwinian hypotheses, or other views characteristic of Western science, but should merely scrutinize all such views on equal terms with all the available alternatives to them . . .

The ideal of parsimonious detachment is strangely exalted here above many other ideals which seem as relevant or more so. This preference is not itself mysterious. It is a plain expression of 'some special code of morals', namely, that of extreme Enlightenment liberalism. But this code itself is not stated or defended. It is simply taken for granted and used to confine the work of moral philosophy, not just to forms, but to a few very general forms which philosophers hoped to establish as uncontroversial, thus avoiding any uncomfortable involvement in actual moral disputes.[8]

Here the thought-process splits up still further, giving an impersonal division of labour, not only between teacher and pupil, but between the whole sharpening-workshop and all the other departments in the intellectual factory. On this model, philosophy shrinks right away from its traditional business of trying to understand conceptual problems *where they arise* in the jungle of living human thought, and becomes a detached speciality for a few. In order to survive in this role, it would have to persuade other groups to bring their tools to this secluded corner for philosophical sharpening. But why should they? The image of sharpening quite fails to bring out the special reason why philosophy is actually needed. (Again, fascination with the ideal of 'sharpness' has had a most misleading influence.) This model suggests very small adjustments, easily contained within other forms of thought.

Likening concepts to tools can indeed be useful, but the point of doing it is exactly to mark out the special role of philosophy as the much more general, structural one of relating the different kinds of work to be done. Philosophy asks how and where different kinds of tools should be used, suggesting how to adapt them for their various purposes, and to devise new ones. The emotivists' idea of a corporate division of labour, splitting up reasoning between a tribe of uncommitted critics and a separate tribe of uncritical believers, cannot work.

THERAPY FOR THINKERS

What, however, about more personal teaching patterns such as Wittgenstein's? This kind of persuasion has often been represented as therapy, and philosophers who have taken up Wittgenstein's ideas in this sense have been labelled as 'therapeutic positivists'. The medical model is attractive today because it sounds humane, and indeed it clearly is much better than the military and forensic ones. Its implications, however, depend very much on how it is conceived and used. To put it crudely, if I am curing you, then I (like Wittgenstein) am right and you are wrong. My calling this wrongness a disease suggests too that I am diagnosing something worse than just a surface error. Some notion of group-therapy or co-counselling seems to be needed here if we are to avoid a kind of naive arrogance that easily infests the medical model. John Wisdom, who has handled this whole range of questions about the psychology of reasoning with a depth and subtlety of attention that they have seldom had since Plato, can show us, first an example of the crude approach, and then, in his later thinking, the considerations that should take us beyond it.

The crude approach appears in a note on the opening pages of Wisdom's book *Other Minds*.[9] Discussing persistent sceptical doubts about 'whether one can really know what another person is feeling', Wisdom writes:

> The treatment is like psycho-analytic treatment . . . in that the treatment is the diagnosis and the diagnosis is the description, the very full description, of the symptoms . . . When in psycho-analysis it is said of a patient, 'He is like this because when he was a child he wished for sexual contact with his mother', this means,
> 'If we analyse him, i.e., let him talk on, he will talk in such and such a way and then feel better'.

It may be said that the analyst cures by recommending a certain view of the patient's case. But the explaining to the patient what is wrong with him consists in allowing the patient to describe his own case . . .

The man who asked the question was best placed for answering it.

In the same way, every philosophical question . . . when it is fully asked, answers itself.

This passage might sound like a recipe for shifting all opponents away from any philosophical position by simply letting them talk themselves out of it until they 'feel better' – that is, more comfortable – somewhere else. Since an immense variety of things can from time to time make people feel better and more comfortable in argument, this seems unduly reductive. Of course, this account echoes the naive confidence of early psycho-analysts in the infallible convergence of the patient's talk, the analyst's theories, and the cure. Questions about the correctness of theories were supposed to be answered simply by the cure. The patient's free associations were not expected either to fail to bear out the analyst's theories, or to fail to cure the patient.

Wisdom accordingly writes here as if, in the sceptic's case, there were no need of actual arguments to show that persistent doubts were meaningless. He runs together the sound point, that the 'patients' themselves must generate thoughts that give real ground to their conviction, with the irrelevant point that they must themselves produce (parthenogenetically) the arguments that convince them, and he assumes either that those arguments will always be forthcoming or that they are needless. In early psycho-analytic models, the analyst's theoretical contribution was consistently under-estimated in this way. Strong characters like Freud overlooked their own influence and supposed that they had told the patient nothing. Teachers, too, can be similarly deluded. In this way an unreal ideal of 'non-directiveness' arises, generating elaborate pretences which greatly increase confusion. If this is extended further into discussion that is not meant to be teaching at all – if I set about curing you of your errors without being asked to and without mentioning them, merely by psychological strategy – then I am probably treating you dishonestly, and I certainly lose all chance of learning from you if, after all, you happen to be right.

Wisdom went on to deal admirably with these difficulties, giving plenty of solid arguments for the meaninglessness of sceptical doubts, and directing the therapeutic techniques that he still favoured much more discriminatingly to areas where there was special reason to suspect neurotic motivation.[10] Moreover, he pointed out that such bracingly reductive accounts as he had here given of scepticism tend to show 'that disrespect for other people which, we may platitudinously say, so often damages philosophical work. A disrespect which blinds one to the puzzles they raise'.[11] He goes on:

> I want to stress the philosophical usefulness of metaphysical surprises such as 'We can never really know the causes of our sensations'. Wittgenstein allows importance to these theories. They are for him expressions of deep-seated puzzlement . . . But this is not enough . . .
>
> He too much represents them as merely symptoms of linguistic confusion. I wish to represent them as also symptoms of linguistic penetration.
>
> Wittgenstein gives the impression that philosophical remarks either express puzzlement or, if not, are remarks such as Wittgenstein himself makes with a view to curing puzzlement.
>
> This naturally gives rise to the question, *If the proper business of philosophy is the removal of puzzlement, would it not be best done by giving a drug to the patient which made him entirely forget the statements puzzling him, or at least lose his uneasy feelings?*[12] [Emphasis mine.]

This shows up admirably the weaknesses of the therapeutic model. The medical art is restorative, presupposing a clear notion of normal health as a former satisfactory state to be regained. But the central reason why philosophy has become necessary at all is that perfectly normal, healthy thought can run into problems that are too hard for it, so that it must change itself. Certainly bad thinking can intensify these problems, and correcting it is a central part of philosophical business. But the idea which Wittgenstein often favoured (especially in his early work), that philosophizing itself is the disease, that ordinary thought would be quite all right if only philosophers didn't interfere with it, is a wild one.

Wisdom, moving steadily away from this naive position, pointed more and more towards a model based on a much more sophisticated idea of psycho-analytic enquiry, an idea which its great practitioners too certainly held – not as a snap journey back to 'feeling better', but as a quest for deeper understanding of our own motivation, broadening into an understanding of our whole human predicament:

In the labyrinth of metaphysics are the same whispers as one hears when climbing Kafka's staircases to the tribunal which is always one floor further up . . . We may hurry away and drown the cries that follow from those silent places . . . But if we can't, we must return, force the accusers to speak up, and insist on recognizing the featureless faces. We can hardly do this for ourselves. But there are those who will go with us and, however terrifying the way, not desert us.[13]

Philosophy, in short, is at root not a neurotic aberration but a quest for self-knowledge as an aspect of understanding the world, a quest made necessary not just by illness of any kind but by the direct need for that understanding. Thus the therapeutic model, at its deepest, converges with the educational one, and in both the main work is seen to be done by the learner in collaboration with outside helpers. The objectionable, extraneous figure of the brain-surgeon or ingot-placer evaporates. I do not think that this or any other single model sums up the whole truth about this or any other study. But in enlightened form, it is one of a family of helpful images, by whose help we can hope to resist some of the miasmas produced by the bad ones.[14]

5

THE USE AND USELESSNESS
OF LEARNING

—— ·◆· ——

THE PROBLEM OF PRIORITIES

How useless are we scholars? How useless ought we to be? Those of us engaged in the less obviously bread-producing enquiries – philosophy, history, pure science, literature and the rest – have to face these questions afresh today. Answers to them which used to be taken for granted are so no longer. Those who control the flow of money have for some time been moving steadily towards a predominant, even a sole reliance on simple, often very short-term economic considerations. That tendency is widespread in the modern world. Sometimes, perhaps, it is just an understandable response of over-worked administrators to the complexity of the choices before them. Any simple, quantitative criterion – for example, the prospect of commercial profitability within five years – looks welcome to them. Criteria of this kind are so convenient that their force in the administrative machine is now enormous. Yet behind this pragmatic acceptance the attitude also has some ideological backing both from right-wing and left-wing theorists. It is not something that will simply go away. It needs to be explicitly thought about.

There is indeed something appealing about the mere simplicity of the thought that concentrating on immediate prospects of profit is common-sense, bypassing all the problems and releasing us from artificial complication. But to hope for such simplicity seems strangely optimistic. No sane person, even in the Mafia, runs their own life by calculations of short-term monetary profit. Though the early classical economists did sometimes hold out such hopes, their more realistic successors have always stressed that economics can at best only be seen as a narrow abstraction from human affairs, never properly intelligible without its wider background. 'Economic man' is a convenient ideal figure, not a complete representation of actual people. And even within this limited economic sphere, only the simple-minded would always favour short-term bargains.

That obvious fact has been obscured a good deal of late by the rhetoric of 'survivalism' – by suggesting that our situation has already reached the simplicity of desperation. In extreme emergencies, such as earthquake, famine or total war, choices do become simplified in this way. Everything is sacrificed for immediate food and shelter. But that is not where we now stand. The painful complexity of our current choices stems rather from the richness of our resources, which presents a constant series of possible options. Financial pressures have *not* reached the point where it makes sense to burn the Titians along with the floorboards and to eat seed corn, or to melt down all the saucepans to make fighter planes.

Choices about funding for various areas of knowledge must therefore be made, and made by discriminating. What principles should decision-makers consider in doing this? What should be saved and what let go? Are there clear signs marking out more valuable from less valuable kinds of knowledge? Certain stereotyped antitheses, attractive from their very simplicity, easily present themselves for this purpose, and can often be used almost unthinkingly by people who have to make a quick decision. These crude antitheses centre on an important ambiguity in the notion of 'use', and on another less obvious but equally serious one in the notion of knowledge. If these ambiguities are not noticed, discussion soon becomes unintelligible.

Attempts to settle priorities among different studies tend to start from a stereotyped opposition between 'useful' and 'useless' knowledge. The point is not always put so crudely, but it is best to use this crude language, since this is the real meaning lying behind such cautious terms as 'sub-optimal', 'disbenefit', 'efficiency' and 'input–output ratio'. This general antithesis can then be interpreted in various ways, for instance as showing that we should always prefer

1 means to ends, or
2 natural sciences to the humanities, or
3 commissioned to spontaneous studies, or
4 revolutionary to traditional approaches.

Let us consider these stereotypes in turn.

MEANS AND ENDS

We sometimes speak of 'use' in quite a wide sense, giving it almost the same range as 'point' or 'value'. We then talk of the use that (say) music or friendship has for us, meaning the point of it, the deep role that it plays in our lives. (Thus Shakespeare wrote, 'Sweet are the uses of adversity.') What is useless in this sense does us no direct good at all; it has no value. But at other times, and perhaps more often, the word has a narrower sense; 'useful' things are then just things like tools or machines which we view simply as means, not expected to have any value in themselves.

But the two senses may get mixed. To say that music or friendship is not 'useful' in the second sense can then seem to mean that it is also useless in the first sense – valueless. (Of course these things may happen to have value as means too; music may drive off rats or cure one's migraine. But to discuss their value only in these terms would be quite misleading.) Under this confused light, the whole value system becomes distorted. Work is then still valued as a means to ends which will be pursued in leisure, but leisure itself is seen as containing only slight, frivolous occupations, lacking the weight which gives solid reality to the world of work. Hence came the notorious problem of the Victorian self-made industrialist, who no longer knew how to use or enjoy the wealth he had collected, because he no longer found anything but the work itself worth doing. Everything else had lost its value.

This confusion about the status of ends still disturbs our lives and distorts our priority systems today. The fanatical concentration on means which leads to neglect of ends is now often flatteringly described as 'Utilitarianism', but this is a euphemism. Calling something utilitarian seems to concede that it is actually useful. Besides, the real utilitarian philosophers (Bentham and Mill) laid great stress on ultimate ends – on the pleasure or happiness finally aimed at – and rejected short-term thinking. Another name sometimes given to the attitude is the 'Protestant work ethic'. There is some historical sense in this, since Protestant doctrines have indeed often been used as a justification by the propagandists and pioneers of the Industrial Revolution. But Protestantism is after all a form of Christianity. The fierce contempt of Jesus for this subjugation of ends to means was explicit. ('What shall it profit a man if he gain the whole world and lose his soul?' and 'Thou fool, this day shall thy soul be required of thee').

EFFORT, REWARD AND VALUE

A better name for the current blind devotion to the immediate balance-sheet is *philistinism* – meaning not just bad taste in aesthetic matters, but a general obtuseness about human values, emotional numbness and blindness, sheer insensitive neglect of the range of valuable experience. In economic parlance, it is *short-termism*, which serious economists themselves deplore.

In explaining the point of the intellectual life today, we have to spell out the drawbacks of philistinism plainly, because we are often speaking to people (such as Thatcherites) who officially accept it – who have, in fact, signed up for an intellectual fashion which calls on them to overlook the price that has to be paid for their financial gambles in the general numbing of human faculties. It is not necessarily a waste of time to talk to these people, because all such fashions are changeable and occupy only a part of the mind. But it does mean that we must ourselves be quite clear about what we are claiming, and must make that claim as clear as possible to bystanders who are considering whether to join this fashion or not.

Applied to knowledge, this confused philistine approach divides it sharply into

1 *means*, bits of information that can be used to secure prosperity and thereby leisure, and
2 *useless elements*, serving only for amusement, which are enjoyed as a hobby when leisure arrives.

Put plainly like this, such a notion may seem somewhat grotesque, but the ideas behind it are quite powerful today, and we need to spell out what is actually wrong with them.

The central trouble is that this scheme simply leaves no room for ends. Instead, there is an unrealistic atomizing of human experience which radically divides reward from effort. A satisfying life does not really work on the pattern of 'jam tomorrow', constantly using neutral, tedious means to secure a later reward. Instead, it calls for networks of activity which are self-rewarding as a whole – which constitute ends in themselves. There are obvious and familiar examples in the arts, in work and in personal relations. The relation of means to these larger ends is that of part to whole.

Moreover, knowledge itself is not an aggregate of separate atoms, bits of information, each valued simply so far as it is a means to producing later reward. Knowledge is primarily a matter of understanding. As Einstein said, 'Knowledge exists in two forms – lifeless, stored in books, and alive, in the consciousness of men'.[1]

Understanding is a pattern of comprehension within which particular facts find their place and help to make sense out of an otherwise confused whole. This kind of pattern is also, incidentally, very useful as a means to further ends. But besides that, it is something strongly and directly desired. Knowledge can reasonably be seen as an end in itself simply because people find confusion so painful and destructive. They need understanding, not just in order to make their livings, but also in order to make their lives worthwhile.

When, in Chapter 1, I quoted Socrates' saying that 'the unexamined life is unliveable for man',[2] I pointed out that he was not making an exaggerated claim for the importance of academic studies. He was simply drawing attention to this human pattern-seeking tendency, this making sense of the mess. And although academic work is now intensely specialized in detail, there are always scholars and writers with the urge to synthesize as well as analyse. We all share in the general understanding of life that flows from the immense collective enterprise.

The ideas we live by and take for granted are in large part those painfully devised by earlier generations of original thinkers. As I said in Chapter 1, Shelley was right when he wrote that poets are the unacknowledged legislators of mankind, but they are not the only ones. They are often the first to articulate ideas that are beginning to be needed, but they are not alone in doing so. Ideas worked out in every branch of the intellectual scene can influence our lives profoundly, both for good and ill.

In the natural sciences, the Copernican revolution that removed the earth from the centre of the universe has had an immense influence on our everyday thinking, and so has the biological theory of evolution. Again, our sense of the historical process that has formed us has been shaped by generations of careful historians, and it contributes in all kinds of unnoticed ways to make possible the thoughts that we need today. Philosophy, again, has continually worked to formulate the conceptual schemes underlying both thought and life, and to make it possible to change them when that is needed. Large ideas are living things, parts of the life around them, and they need to grow and develop as the rest of it does so. They cannot do this only at the public, visible level. An immense amount of background thought and research – some of it quite technical – is needed to make possible the new thinking of people who will never hear of that detailed work at all.

THE PLACE OF KNOWLEDGE IN LIFE

I have been pointing out the absurdity of supposing that only things useful as means are valuable, and stressing the importance of knowledge as an end. What, however, follows from this when we consider priorities? To say that something is an end in itself does not of course mean that it is the only end, nor that it necessarily takes precedence over other ends. Human beings need many other things besides knowledge. In order to examine the value of any single aim properly we have to sketch out some sort of priority system relating it to those other aims with which it may compete.

Many defences of the intellectual life are weakened by failing to notice this need. It is not enough simply to say, as is often done, that human beings are naturally curious, that 'man has always longed to penetrate the mysteries of nature' and so forth, because plenty of cultures, and plenty of people in our own culture, are content with very limited access to this ideal. It is even less convincing to claim, as Jacques Monod did, that scientific enquiry is the only thing that has objective value, in a world from which all other value has mysteriously been drained.[3] This is merely to exalt one's own preferences arbitrarily in a way that people whose tastes are different have no reason to accept. Partial, imperialistic claims of this kind, insisting on supremacy for one particular branch of thought, can always be answered with equal conviction from another. Thus Iris Murdoch:

> Words are the most subtle symbols that we possess and our human fabric depends on them . . . It is totally misleading to speak, for instance, of 'two cultures', one literary–humane and the other scientific, as if these were of equal status. There is only one culture, of which science, so interesting and so dangerous, is now an important part. But the most essential and fundamental aspect of culture is the study of literature, since this is an education in how to picture and understand human situations. We are men and we are moral agents before we are scientists, and the place of science in human life must be discussed in *words*. This is why it is and always will be more important to know about Shakespeare than to know about any scientist, and if there is a Shakespeare of science his name is Aristotle.[4]

The difference between these two manifestos is that Iris Murdoch gives plenty of reasons for her contention. And so far as they establish the importance of literature they are indeed good reasons. But it is surely a mistake to think that this involves any downgrading of science. The concerns are different, they are simply not in competition. The row about supremacy which convulsed the 'two cultures' debate in the 1960s was misconceived. What is needed is for all the separate branches of thought to understand their own function, and relate it to the whole.

This effort is not helped by Jacques Monod's tactic of shouting that the supreme valuation of science is simply an inescapable, ultimate existential choice. Irrationalist rhetoric of this vague kind has done harm to the serious cause of defending the search for knowledge. Human beings are indeed to some extent naturally curious, and do seek to understand the world around them. But no other civilisation has given this project anything like the high priority that we have found for it in our own, nor carried it anything like so far. Other societies stress other values; many of them would certainly find this particular intellectual bias puzzling.

DO WE WANT TO SEE THE WOOD OR THE TREES?

If we do want to say why we should value knowledge particularly highly, the most obvious and uncontroversial reason is that we are already committed to it. Modern Western life depends on complex kinds of knowledge. We have, so to speak, already got so far into the forest that there is little point now in starting to ask whether that is where we really want to be. It is important, however, for people not to drop the subject once this purely practical point is established, but to ask themselves also whether they do value knowledge in some way *as an end in itself.* If they do not, then they are beginning to dismantle a structure of values which has so far been central in our culture.

Changes of this sort can of course be made, but people who propose to make them need to do so openly and consciously, not casually and by mistake. If, too, this dismantling is not meant to be a mere process of disintegration, like that which overtook American Indian communities when their traditional way of life was shattered, it is essential to explain what new ideals are to take the place of those which are to be downgraded. The analogy of the forest describes our inner predicament as well as our outer, practical one. We belong to modern Western culture spiritually as well as physically, and cannot turn ourselves into different kinds of beings without answering to the ideals we propose to desert.

Thoughtful people have long had a sense that knowledge does have this kind of importance, but the reasons for this have not of late been spelt out in a way that could make them available at once when the whole position was threatened. To do this we need to ask sharply,

'What sort of an end do we take knowledge to be? Do we value it chiefly as understanding, as contemplation which is the soul's proper activity, or have the mere collecting and storing of information high value in themselves?' Talk of 'man's natural curiosity' often does not distinguish these elements. Curiosity may mean no more than the burning desire to answer particular, isolated factual questions – for instance, about what is in Pandora's box or in Bluebeard's room. This kind of desire is undoubtedly a strong human tendency, and sometimes, though by no means always, a valuable one. But it plainly is not the main motivation here. Even when particular questions do obsess us – for instance, when we ask 'who killed Olof Palme?' or 'exactly what happened at the Big Bang?' – they do not stand alone. We are looking for an explanation of some much larger range of puzzles.

Some accounts (such as Monod's) tend to suggest that the all-justifying aim of enquiry is simply to get at the truth – any truth. There is, of course, great force in this if we think of truth in contrast to being deceived. But some truths are trivial. Simply counting the pebbles in my back garden is not a valuable aim. Truth that is worth pursuing needs to contribute to understanding.

BEING PREPARED

If this is what we want to stress, it makes a great difference to the meaning of education. Gaining knowledge is not just collecting and storing facts, but becoming trained in handling them. We need practice in using many different methods, so that an effective education needs to mention whole ranges of facts that are quite different from those among which a student is liable to live and work. The reason why those in their final years at school may be asked to study *Othello* and the differential calculus and the geography of the Antarctic is not that anyone expects them to confront Renaissance Italians doing mathematics at the South Pole, but to develop their general understanding of the world they live in. They are being supplied with a set of rough maps – physical, emotional and intellectual – of central ranges of human experience, maps which they will later extend, refine and fill in for themselves.

When shortages loom, educational authorities naturally try to prune away all teaching that is not part of a direct training for work, work that society will value enough to pay wages for. But if the general development of people's faculties is neglected beyond a certain point, they often become too depressed, alienated and discouraged to take in even the narrow training that can make them fit for this work. The general power of receiving particular trainings constructively is itself something which needs its own kind of training and cherishing.

Adolescents who have not managed to develop these faculties in the course of education will develop them on their own, and will insist on finding a meaning for their lives on lines which may indeed be valuable, but may also range from soccer hooliganism through bizarre religious and political movements to drug-taking, despair and suicide. Less dramatically, they may just give up and retreat into dull inertia. Although there are limits to what education can do to put meaning into people's lives, it must surely be part of the business of educators to help people to make sense of the world around them, and so to find ways of life that are acceptable to others and also worthwhile for themselves. To treat this function as a mere luxury would imply a very strange idea of usefulness.

THE 'TWO CULTURES'

The ideas just sketched have of course underlain the humanistic education prevalent in Europe since the Renaissance. Classical studies were supposed to be used to develop students' faculties and characters, in a style that has since been extended through the rest of 'the humanities', by immersion in European languages, literature, history and philosophy.

This humanistic tradition had many strengths, but its weakness has been its neglect of other studies, in particular of the natural sciences. Those sciences originally had a place in the educational system, but that place was not properly enlarged (especially in Britain) to keep pace with their rapid growth and increasing independence in the nineteenth century. As they expanded, these sciences became associated with technology in a way that made them seem to the general public more 'useful', and tended to save scientists the trouble of explaining why, at a deeper level, their discoveries mattered in themselves. The final professionalization of scientific studies gave them the status of independent specialities, but it did not really integrate them again with the humanistic educational enterprise. The social sciences similarly developed somewhat apart from the traditional intellectual centre.

Thus there grew up a division between the arts or humanities and 'science' – far sharper in England than in most European countries, in the United States or indeed in Scotland. Because science now gained great prestige, this meant that the traditional justifications of learning, which had centred on the humanities, were in some degree forgotten. It led to a further and still more unfortunate widening of the tribal division between scientists and humanists, establishing the second antithesis on our list. Science (both physical and social) was typecast as useful but somewhat vulgar, while humanism prided itself on being beautiful but – in the second sense I have noted for that word – useless.

HOLIER THAN THOU AND EVEN MORE USELESS

In the 1960s, the absurdly confrontational 'two cultures' debate accordingly displayed these two complementary aspects of life as rivals contending for some imaginary despotic position.[5] It is true that in a sense there is only one culture, but disputes of this sort expose distinct sub-cultures – groups of people with their own customs and patriotic noises, who do not bother to understand each other. This particular feud was doubly absurd because the borderline between the two supposed contenders was itself obscure.

On which side should we place logic, geography, archaeology, musicology, mathematics? G.H. Hardy's famous and impressive claim that mathematics was useless[6] seemed to demand for it a share in the peculiar kind of unworldly honour that was earmarked for the classics. Similarly, George Steiner in his striking Bronowski Lecture 'Has Truth a Future?' declared more generally that the mark of a true scholar is 'his addiction . . . with the abstract, the inapplicable, the sovereignly useless'.[7]

This paradoxical line of talk can be pretty misleading if it is not carefully explained, and it is increasingly ill-understood today. (Thus, a speaker at the World Congress of Philosophy in August 1988 who said that philosophy was useless – meaning that it did not necessarily have to improve the trade balance – was widely reported by the press as having accepted that it was an indefensible occupation.) By contrast, the social sciences, which occupy the other major borderline in this simple art/science division, are sometimes accepted, with a faith that may seem a little surprising, as instrumentally useful – though there is more scepticism about this than there used to be in the case of sociology. And again, in so far as they seemed useful as means, they have not been asked to justify their existence so often as the humanities have.

This whole feud has been doubly disastrous. Scientists have tended to lose confidence and interest in the studies which might have linked their own work to the rest of life such as the history of science.

Humanists meanwhile, by remaining ignorant of science, have lost an apprehension and admiration of the physical world which ought, by their own standards, to form at least as central a part of their equipment for life as the knowledge of human history. Human history itself cannot be properly understood without some grasp of the workings of the physical world in which its dramas are played out. But beyond this (as philosophers as well as scientists have stressed), natural science is for its students an enlightening vision, a form of contemplation which, equally with the arts, can properly serve as the centre of a full human life. Goethe was – deservedly – as famous in his own day for his pioneering work in comparative anatomy as for his poetry. Aristotle, Descartes and Kant shared this wider vision with Darwin and Einstein, and its loss from our local humanistic tradition has been a disaster.

I have been considering the first two crude notions of 'uselessness' which I mentioned, and have noted the way in which they are intertwined. To resist their misleading effects, a vigorous dialogue is needed between the arts and sciences, and also within each particular discipline, to make us all clearer about just why what we are doing is valuable. For all intellectual enquiries, the narrow notion of 'use' that confines it to *means* is a disaster. It ignores the clear sense in which (say) music and poetry are useful to us, when we use them as the focus and framework of our deepest experiences. These things have a direct value for us, and so does science. In this sense, use is not an external means to tomorrow's results; it is our direct support and guidance today. Because these activities are aspects of our experience, they are ends in themselves.

As I have suggested, this status does not stop them having valuable results as well. Such activities do tend to be lasting, and also to nourish the whole character. But their good effects in this respect constitute a *secondary* kind of usefulness, a consequence which is not possible unless the primary kind occurs first. Music or information that is not 'used' – in the sense of being fully absorbed and digested in experience – will not normally be of much use in its later effects either. Unimaginative, narrowly technical training in serious subjects produces boredom, pretentiousness and barren imitation, not the fruitful understanding which reshapes experience.

COMMISSIONED OR SPONTANEOUS RESEARCH?

Does this account of educational goals and values extend to research as well? Or is that a radically different kind of occupation? Is research perhaps simply a job – a field where adults whose characters and intellects are already fully formed devote themselves to gathering those facts that the community around them happens to need, whether or no they find these facts interesting in themselves? Is it perhaps quite all right for research to be boring?

Here is our third and perhaps most plausible antithesis – the one between commissioned and spontaneous research. For administrators, this is a most convenient and attractive division. Ought not the questions that get investigated be the ones which somebody other than the investigators already wants answered? And if commercial interests or government agencies already know what information they need, should not their demands be the regular, expected condition for starting – or at least for supporting – any enquiry?

This point is not a silly one, even where research is a voluntary occupation, and today, when it is usually funded by some body or other, it becomes more serious. There is good reason for enquirers to feel a special responsibility to deal with problems that are actually causing trouble in the world. This responsibility becomes stronger, too, in a world which is already an intellectual maze, so much shaped by previous thoughts and theories that it is often hard to find the way out without sharing some part of the education that produced the trouble. This is most obviously true in the physical and social sciences, but it is just as true in literature and philosophy – above all in ethics. The ideas that have shaped our present way of living are so pervasive that they are surprisingly hard to notice, and becoming clearer about them can be of the utmost importance in finding our way forward. Accordingly, one great reason for studying the thought of the past, and of other cultures, is that it gives us a perspective from which we can actually see and criticize the ideas that we have grown up with.

This does place some responsibility on those who get such an education to use it for the common good – to direct their thoughts towards problems with some practical bearing. English-speaking philosophy is now returning to such problems after a long and tedious vacation in which its practitioners spoke only to each other, and this is a most welcome change.

THE NEED FOR SPECIALIZATION

All the same, learning can never be confined to these problems. The nature of thought is to produce large systems, to ramify far beyond our ordinary knowledge and our ordinary attention-span. There always has to be an enormous hidden background. This background is constantly accused of being trivial, and the reply must always be that it is as necessary as the floorboards we walk on, even though it is just as unobtrusive. The great Greek scholar Porson said that he 'would be content if men hereafter knew that there had lived, towards the end of the eighteenth century, one Porson, who did a good deal for the text of Euripides'. And he was right to think so. What he did for that text was quite simply to make it intelligible again – to clear away, by detailed criticism, a great mass of textual corruptions and in so doing to rediscover the lost and forgotten workings of the metre, so that the sound of poetry (not just of Euripides but of all the Greek dramatists) could in some degree be heard again.

What that did for all of us whose lives have been shaped by that poetry and the ideas behind it is inestimable. We owe a great deal, too, to translators and to scholars such as Gilbert Murray who have worked at a level nearer to ordinary thought. But their work would be impossible without the hard technical grind of people like Porson. Similarly, it is not possible to philosophize effectively about current problems without using the methods forged by deeper and more comprehensive thinkers – and if one is going to use them, one had better understand them.

There is a painful dialectic here between the need for technical thoroughness and the need to make thought available to structure the common experience. This dialectic we need to face. Scholars in this century have been inclined to avoid it by diving hastily into specialization in an effort to impress each other. It gets harder and harder today to make an academic career if one does not do this. That bias has made it much easier for philistines to undercut them, to bypass their whole enterprise and dismiss it as trivial, demanding only research that is 'relevant', meaning immediately profitable. This is not only foolish; it is also a lost cause. There is no way of knowing in advance which research is going to make money, nor even (more respectably) which research will solve a particular problem, such as controlling inflation or finding a cure for AIDS.

WE'LL KNOW WHAT WE'RE LOOKING FOR WHEN WE FIND IT

There is enormous difficulty in finding what line of enquiry will best meet a particular need. The search for knowledge differs from nearly every other kind of search in that, until it succeeds, the searchers can have no clear idea just what it is that they are searching for. That is the quite peculiar difficulty besetting this whole topic. Commissioning bodies, whether public or private, are in principle as much at sea about it as anyone else. They naturally tend to continue whatever line of thought has lately been prevalent. In this way, however, they have sometimes, with the best of intentions, wasted great resources on false trails – for example, the Special Cancer Virus Program in President Nixon's 'War on Cancer'.

This difficulty is naturally even greater when the discovery that is actually needed is a particularly large and unexpected one – a situation which, from its very nature, cannot be identified in advance. The big, crucial discoveries that have made possible the astonishing technical advances of the last two centuries, such as those of Faraday and Clerk Maxwell about electricity, have nearly all been made by people who were not actually directing their thoughts to practical applications. Again, the science of ecology has been gradually built up by biologists who were at least as often moved by specific curiosity or the wish to understand first principles as by the prospect of practical application. Thus James Lovelock made the first observations that alerted English-speaking scientists in the 1960s to the dangers of atmospheric pollution because, while on holiday in Ireland, he was curious about the cause of an unexpected haze and used instruments of his own devising to measure the minute traces of the chemical compounds that caused it. Few people, until very lately, ever thought of ecology as an insurance against disaster, and even fewer were prepared to fund it as such.

In the humanities, things look slightly different because we do not think so much in terms of sudden great 'discoveries' casting dramatic new lights on the scene. But this difference is not really as great as it may seem. In the first place, science itself does not really advance so much by the sudden unveiling of large particular facts as by the development of new ways of thinking. And the effect of new ways of thinking can be just as striking in other fields.

Nobody commissioned Hobbes or Rousseau or Kant to develop social-contract theory as a solution to the political problems of their age, or Hegel to invent the organic theory of the State. But after they had made these conceptual shifts, everything began to look different. And in the follow-up to these large changes, a host of minor ones is needed, equally in the arts and sciences, to work out the implications, which is where research comes in. Thus, neither in the arts nor in the sciences is there progress up a kind of staircase, jumping from one Nobel Prize winner to the next. Big conceptual shifts have to be continually reinterpreted in every age. And someone who thus reinterprets one of these writers today may be finding a way to help with our present difficulties about democracy – a way which would never occur to people who remained resolutely contemporary.

In sum, there is no doubt that, if researchers had followed a strict policy of pursuing only work that could already be seen to be useful, the new thoughts just mentioned and innumerable others equally vital would never have developed. This conclusion, however, is not so unconstructive as it may sound in our search for priorities. Though it is true that no one can tell at what point in the field a crucial view will crop up, it is not true that nobody knows what sort of field to cultivate in order to make its appearance possible. Plainly, what is needed to make room for it is a wide range, a rich, fertile and varied background of study and thought.

VARIETY IS NOT A LUXURY

Evolutionary metaphors are quite appropriate here. If a species is to adapt to changing circumstances where new challenges may constantly confront it, it needs a wide and varied gene-pool which will give it a reasonable chance of throwing up mutations that can meet any particular challenge. Indeed, even for mere survival without new challenges, a much wider gene-pool is needed than might be thought, because too narrow a range of individuals will not be able to spread out so as to exploit a particular environment effectively. Without exceptional good luck, monocultures spell ecological disaster. Variety is not a luxury, it is not just the spice of life; it is an essential condition of survival, and this is every bit as true of the intellectual life as it is of the biological one.

It is worthwhile to pause for a moment on this evolutionary metaphor, because misuse of it has done much to produce the ways of thinking that underlie current mistakes. The idea that revivifying any enterprise will normally (and not just sometimes) be a matter of 'slimming' it, by starving it and forcing it to compete more sharply with others, seems to draw much support from the notion that biological evolution works entirely by sharpening competition in a way that ensures what Herbert Spencer called the 'survival of the fittest'. This naive notion startlingly overlooks the fact that much the commonest effect of such sharpened competition is to produce extinctions or, in milder cases, to drive a species to a less prosperous way of life. The usual effect of starvation is death. Something survives, but not necessarily the species in question.

69

It is time to cash the evolutionary metaphor. What do we mean by saying that a wide background of thought is needed if valuable discoveries are to emerge? Why should such a background be necessary? It is so because *the progress of thought is never a straight line, in which one problem simply appears behind another and all can be solved by the same method.* Though our natural laziness makes us constantly hope that we can apply this pattern, it never works for long. Different methods are continually being needed, and approaches other than those currently favoured have constantly to be brought in as correctives.

It is perhaps in an effort to resist this ossifying tendency that people sometimes turn to the last antithesis on our list, and assume that what is new will necessarily be more useful than what is old. The hope then is that it will be possible to supply just the new ideas that are needed, while getting rid of the out-of-date ones. The trouble about this project is that valuable ideas normally arise organically out of a wide, many-sided, undisturbed range of ongoing background work. It is a mistake to be hypnotized by Nobel Prizes into supposing that their proud possessors stand alone.

Faraday was building on a century of international research on electricity and magnetism. Hobbes and Rousseau were only nodes in a long, ancient, constructive discussion about the possibility of social contracts. To use and develop the new ideas involves integrating them into existing ways of thinking and letting them interact so that they fertilize one another. Intellectual progress cannot be conducted by replacing one whole population of ideas and principles with another, as an executive might decide to buy a set of new plants for his office. It needs to develop as a whole ecosystem.

CONCLUSION: WHAT IS KNOWLEDGE FOR?

In this chapter, I have said a little about the general notion of usefulness, which surely needs much sharper criticism than it is getting today. I have been concentrating on the special case of knowledge. I have suggested that its value must lie centrally, not just in the possessing and storing of information as a means to something else, but in understanding, in the power to systematize and use that information in large-scale thinking and so in our lives. Though 'use' is often practical, it also involves first and foremost an inner, contemplative element, constitutive of what we are.

Knowledge is not just loose facts, it is understanding. If the search for it were no more than the gathering of certain isolated, applicable bits of information, it might make sense to collect only those ones, perhaps on the analogy of mining jewels. But the situation is more like the cultivation of a garden or the development of our own faculties. It relies on wide-ranging and cumulative practice. Pianists cannot economically bypass all other elements in their art and acquire, by careful cost-benefit analysis, only the tricks they need to play the *Appassionata*. In the case of learning, the background of practice needs to be wide, social, interactive, informed by basic trust, and essentially co-operative rather than competitive. Paradoxically, we need to know much more than we shall ever need to know.

Though curiosity is certainly a general human tendency, the special aspiration after a fully methodical understanding of the whole universe, which has been a peculiar choice of our culture, could be abandoned at any time. Indeed, since it requires strenuous and con-tinued effort, merely ceasing to take trouble about it could easily destroy it. If we let this happen, we would be disclaiming and drop-ping this special kind of interest. Even if, less drastically, we only compromise by starving and underfunding it, as we in Britain are doing at present, we declare to our children that it is not an enter-prise that will be worth their while to enter.

Knowledge is not something that we have and can buy; it is some-thing that we do and are. Without such understanding, knowledge obtained from others is useless in every sense. If our countries choose reliance on this second-hand stuff, they are opting to stop trying to grasp at first hand certain essential aspects of the world, aspects which up to now we have considered vital. If our rulers really no longer value these, that remarkable change in priorities ought to be stated openly and – if any defence is possible – explicitly defended.

6

SEX AND PERSONAL IDENTITY

—— .◆. ——

INDIVIDUALISM RUNS into particular difficulties over the topic of gender because theorists always find it hard to admit that human beings, like other animals, come in two kinds. This shyness has contributed a good deal more than is often noticed to the distortion of our individualistic tradition. The topic is genuinely tricky, because the sex difference is not quite like any other difference. Many current intellectual approaches tend to treat it as just one among many differences of power and status.

This will not do. Neither bland eighteenth-century formulas based on equality – on the hope that, foolish prejudice apart, men and women will turn out to be just the same – nor attempts to hijack the Marxist formula of the class struggle, with women playing the part of the proletariat, will fit the case. Power and status do raise real problems. But they could never have done so had there not in the first place been a deeper, much more mysterious difference in kind, making people in all human cultures fall into two groups according to gender. Failure to think about this difference muddles our whole notion of a human being.

DIFFERENT DIFFERENCES

The reason why we find it hard to grasp this painfully obvious point is that our moral and political tradition lacks slots for differences in kind. Where it sees difference, it tends to see hierarchy, making divisions into better and worse. This is as true of Left-wing as of Right-wing thinking, and it is the reason why the current attachment of feminism to the Left is getting us nowhere. This is not, of course, to say that attachment to the Right would be any better. The crude and confused Left–Right antithesis brackets together sets of policies whose connection can often only be understood by a careful tracing of political history. It never helps us in trying to think about new issues. And an issue which most thinkers in our main tradition have flatly refused to think about at all has to be counted as a new one.

Why do we find it so hard to think about it? The difficulty is not just the natural reluctance of a privileged group to surrender power. If it were only that, all women would find the issue quite simple, and they do not. The wider trouble is that our whole intellectual and social tradition centres at present on the idea of an individual, and that individual is conceived as male. The individualist tradition, being supposedly radical and universal, demands to be extended to females, but it is so constructed that it cannot be. The tone of the tradition has always been rationalistic; stark, honest realism is its watchword. But evasion, partiality and self-deception have always eroded it on this central issue – central not just because it affects half the human race, but because the other half too cannot be thought about honestly in isolation.

MEN ON WIMMIN

It is therefore not surprising that, on the one hand, a great jumble of problems involving women piles up for our attention, brought forward by a great variety of reformers, loosely grouped under the name of feminists; nor is it surprising, on the other, that many people come to hate the very sound of this name and will go to great lengths to avoid hearing anything about it. How strong this feeling is I only realized lately when I found how people regarded my working on the topic. Philosophers would ask what I was busy with. The year before, the answer was 'animals'; everybody glowed and responded. When I said 'women', however, people tended to sympathize, as if I had named a disease, and to ask respectfully how I could stand it. My reply was roughly that I like confusions – that I find them interesting, especially when they have practical effects, and even more interesting when they are open and flagrant than when a cover-up job has been attempted. My questioners would then agree gravely that in that case I would not be short of work.

It was clear that they expected all these confusions to belong to the feminists, which indeed a great many of them did. But nobody who has not gone into the question would believe how badly the great philosophers themselves perform on this question. It is not just that some of what they say about women is false, nor even that some of it is wicked. What startles is its silliness. When this topic is raised, normal standards of thought collapse. The Enlightenment grows dark, while the Christian Fathers, forgetting love, tend to radiate unthinking hatred. It is no pleasure to me to point this out, for I love the great European philosophic tradition. But this is something plain, something which anthropologists visiting the earth from a gender-free planet would find startling and highly significant. Of all the great European philosophers, only Plato and John Stuart Mill try to approach this topic as they would any other – questioning dispassionately, and using their normal powers of criticism.

I cannot document this alarming generalization properly here, though I shall look in a moment at some of those great Enlightenment figures whose muddles on this matter are especially instructive and serious. The point that interests me is of course not to knock the mighty dead, but to notice the difficulty which their failure indicates in what might seem to be a simple subject, and did seem so to them. Many scholars, however, do see this move as an attack, and sweep it aside with an historical broom. They argue that the philosophers simply made a mistake which in their day anybody would have made, so that it is as unfair to blame them for it as for their mistakes about the composition of matter or the shape of the universe. Against blame, that is no doubt a good defence. But blame is not the point. The interesting question is 'What happens if we now correct that mistake? How much difference will it make to the value of the rest of their thought, and to its bearing on life?'

REPLUMBING THE GENDER SYSTEM

Mistakes about the physical world can often be corrected without much effect on the surrounding thoughts. How do we do this about women? To historical-minded dismissers, the job looks quite simple. We shall just take out one section of conceptual piping and replace it with a more modern one. We drop the old, crude attitude to women and put in instead the enlightened, perfectly satisfactory one which is in use today. This operation, they add, is not really a philosophical one at all, just an application of ready-made philosophy. The ideas themselves are in order, and merely need extending to a new group. A typical case would be a brisk revision of the voting register. Others, equally simple, would follow, such as extending the educational system and making all marriage laws perfectly symmetrical . . .

Obviously, however, if that were all, we would not be in the muddle we are in today. Nor would past sages have done so badly. This is not a case of scientific ignorance, cured by some sudden theoretical discovery which makes everything thereafter straightforward. The main concepts involved were on hand in the eighteenth century, and were vigorously applied in other areas. Certainly, since then, there has been a great change in attitudes to women. But it has been a slow, confused and halting one, constantly held up by the awkwardness of its conceptual tools. And not only is it still incomplete, but it has reached an impasse where, without a real revision of those basic working concepts – individuality, autonomy, independence, freedom and the rest – it will jam itself and finally fail.

Let me sum up the matter crudely. The whole idea of a free, independent, enquiring, choosing individual, an idea central to European thought, has always been essentially the idea of a male. It was so developed by the Greeks, and still more by the great libertarian movements of the eighteenth century. In spite of its force and nobility, it contains a deep strain of falsity, not just because the reasons why it was not applied to one half of the human race were not honestly looked at, but because the supposed independence of the male was itself false. It was parasitical, taking for granted the love and service of non-autonomous females (and indeed often of the less enlightened males as well). It pretended to be universal when it was not.

MAN THE HERO (BRING A CUSHION)

Feminism, in fact, is quite simply a response to *virism*, to the unconscious, unhesitating assumption that an individual is always an independent male. Because that assumption has varying results in various areas, feminism takes various forms, which makes it confusing. But that doesn't make the original assumption any more sensible. This equivocal, unrealistic attitude to the mutual dependence central to human life does not just inconvenience women. It falsifies the whole basis of life. Morality becomes a lop-sided melodrama. The virtues and qualities we need for love and service are uncritically despised, while those involved in self-assertion are uncritically exalted (except when it is women who do the asserting).

This kind of bad faith is a particularly crippling fault in the sort of extreme individualism which is generally held to belong to the Left – the near-anarchistic strain which descends from Rousseau through Nietzsche to Sartre. Modern feminists, however, have put a lot of confidence in this tradition, and have not subjected Nietzsche to anything like the well-deserved acid-bath which they have given Freud. (Simone de Beauvoir's influence has been powerful here.) On the Right, such thinking is more widely recognized. Indeed, attempts to understand individualism bring out particularly clearly the uselessness of the Right–Left antithesis. Where, on the political spectrum, ought we to place the unspoken creed which runs: 'I believe only in the independent individual, to refrain from interfering with whom is the prime duty of all the world, especially of women'? If there is such a spectrum, its ends run round behind and join each other.

On the recognized Right, an interesting specimen is Carlyle. After his wife's death, he told Tyndall heart-brokenly 'how loyally and lovingly she had made herself a soft cushion to protect him from the rude collisions of the world.' How could someone whose lifelong theme was heroism, and who held great audiences spellbound by his celebrations of it, possibly make such a claim and such an admission? Why did he need his cushion? Carlyle could take this line because he believed devoutly in the romantic cult of the great man or genius, and had no wish to examine that figure suspiciously for feet of clay. In general, too, clashes between ideals never bothered him much, since he thought consistency rather a fiddling consideration. But he also had a real advantage here over many theorists of his time and ours, because he had never claimed to subscribe to the ideals of the French Revolution.

LIBERTY AND EQUALITY, STRICTLY FOR THE FRATERNITY

Could people who were primarily champions of liberty and equality take the same line about women? It might seem hard, but they managed it. The blindness of all the great architects of libertarian thought (until Mill) to this fascinating issue is, I think, a real piece of bad luck, something which could easily have been otherwise. It is certainly not an historical necessity, as it might perhaps be in a culture where such questions had never been raised. Even in Greece, Euripides and Aristophanes had taken the matter seriously. They reflected controversies which were evidently active in their day, and to which Plato responded in the *Republic* by bold arguments and proposals. Aristotle ignored all this, but in doing so he was deliberately turning his back on it, not acting in innocent ignorance. And by the eighteenth century a good number of upper-class women had for some time been educated. They formed a fair part of the reading public, ran salons which were accepted as important centres for the development of ideas, even wrote influential books. All this, of course, was especially true in France, where lively discussion about their position was common.

This was Rousseau's background. In *The Social Contract*, as we all know, he said that 'man is born free, and everywhere he is in chains.' Rousseau demanded unchainment. Whatever else may be obscure here, we tend to think that we also know who he is talking about – namely, all human beings. We must turn to *Émile*, published at the same time, to discover that he means less than half of them:

> Girls should early be accustomed to restraint, because all their life long they will have to submit to the strictest and most enduring restraints, those of propriety . . . They have, or ought to have, little freedom . . . As a woman's conduct is controlled by public opinion, so is her religion ruled by authority . . . Unable to judge for themselves, they should accept the judgement of father and husband as that of the church.[1]

So much for liberty; what about equality? Are women, for instance, equally entitled to education? Rousseau replies that they must get only the minimum which will make them useful housekeepers and not intolerably boring housemates. Theorists demanding more than this do not realise the fearful dangers involved: such would-be reformers,

> not content to secure [women's] rights, lead them to usurp ours, for to make woman our superior in all the qualities proper to her sex, and to make her our equal in all the rest, what is this but to transfer to the woman the superiority which nature has given to her husband?

So wrote the man who owed his career to the devoted, intelligent, educated encouragement of Mesdames de Warens, d'Épinay and others.

Many things contributed to Rousseau's attitude, among them no doubt the resentment of patronage. But it did not flow from ignorance of other possibilities. He was being deliberately reactionary – resisting proposals which in general his whole basic philosophy demanded, yet which he found intolerable. He managed his resistance by simply retreating, when this topic came up, to the older, hierarchical style of thought which he was busy demolishing, and using a corner of it as a refuge.

Since this older style was still familiar, readers who shared his ambivalence on the matter accepted this strange behaviour gladly, and apparently often did not notice it. The ambiguity of terms like 'man' made it just possible – though still surprising – that devotees of the rights of man, or of 'One Man, One Vote' and similar slogans, should feel themselves to be universal in their sympathies, and yet become angry and derisive whenever women's participation was mentioned.

The odd thing is, not that male domination was retained, but that, in so argumentative an age, no need was felt to defend it intelligibly. It was treated as something which need not, and perhaps should not, ever be seriously discussed. Accordingly, as Mill put it:

> The social subordination of women stands out, an isolated fact in modern social institutions . . . a single relic of an old world of thought and practice exploded in everything else, but retained in the one thing of most universal interest; as if a gigantic dolmen, or temple of Jupiter Olympius, occupied the site of St Paul's and received daily worship, while the surrounding Christian churches were resorted to only on fasts and festivals.[2]

Women were to remain hierarchical, feudal, emotional, and organic. If they ceased to be so, they would endanger the men's enterprise of becoming totally free, equal, autonomous, intellectual and creative.

CAN'T SEE, WON'T SEE

Dolmens of this sort are best maintained by not being mentioned. Rousseau's long, explicit, revealing outburst in the fifth book of *Émile* was not widely imitated. Even its admirers may have noticed uneasily the unmistakable smell of spite and panic which it gives off. Apart from Schopenhauer, whose influential *Essay on Women* outdoes Rousseau in all these respects, most serious theorists chose the safer course of pretending that the topic did not exist. Hobbes perhaps takes the palm here, explaining that the family is

> a little monarchy, whether that family consist of a man and his children, or of a man and his servants, or of a man and his children and his servants together.[3]

Similarly, the word *child* in all serious contexts simply means *boy*, as it does throughout Locke's work on education.

From such books, our alien anthropologists would conclude fairly confidently that women were a small minority – a marginal, outlying, anomalous group, perhaps rather like haemophiliacs or typhoid-carriers, with some peculiarities which called for special social arrangements, but so untypical as not to affect the general shape of society. They would notice that any prolonged reference to them tends to be thought frivolous. In political theory, women are usually only mentioned in clear, sharp directives to keep them out of the central argument. Thus Kant, in the course of an impressive essay to show that political obligation absolutely requires the consent of all the governed, so that all citizens must vote, adds briefly that the only qualification required by a citizen, 'apart, of course, from being an adult male', is that he must have some property or some skill to support himself.[4]

This is the remark of a philosopher deeply committed in general to the principle of consent, and deeply interested in the different ways of understanding and applying it. He also in general hates unargued dogma, and is most scrupulous about giving some argument, good or bad, for all his conclusions. He is writing some twenty years later than Rousseau, when questions about women were receiving even more attention, and not long before the French Revolution – a revolution which he welcomed. There really is something here which needs explaining.

We can take for granted two obvious pieces of the explanation – the reluctance of the privileged to consider surrendering power, and the unwillingness of celibate scholars such as Kant to think about a factor which they have managed to exclude from their lives. But, in so passionately rationalistic an age, better reasons than these are needed for passing up the whole argument.

And there are such reasons. On the theoretical side, the notion of what an individual is (which was central to these people's rationalism) had something wrong with it – a fault which has since become still more glaring, and which would have had to be acknowledged at once if any attempt had been made to apply it to women. Crudely – and we have to be crude here to bring the matter out into the open – the Enlightenment notion showed the individual as essentially an isolated will, guided by an intelligence, arbitrarily connected to a slightly unsatisfactory array of feelings, and lodged, rather by chance, in an equally unsatisfactory human body. Each individual's relation to all others is optional, arranged by contract. It depends on the calculations of the intellect and on aims freely chosen by the will.

SUPERMAN RISES ABOVE IT

Since Kant's time, this picture has become far more extreme, largely through Nietzsche's work in exalting solitude and treating the will as not just the chooser of values, but also their creator. In our own supposedly secular age, this model is not fully recognized as active, but it burgeons unofficially into a startling variety of revealing myths. An interesting set concerns the disconnection of mind from body.

This may not seem appropriate to secular rationalism and voluntarism; it is commonly thought of as part of religion. But because the body evidently supplies the basis for the feelings, those who want to exalt intellect and will over feeling also need to make a sharp division here. They draw their model from Descartes, usually now rejecting his view that the soul is immortal, but keeping its independence of the body. That very significant thing, science fiction, expresses this myth currently in many forms, reincarnating consciousness in all sorts of alternative bodies, natural or mechanical, and sometimes even dodging death.

Real scientists too are influenced by these notions; indeed, one Dean E. Wooldridge offers to put the scheme into practice. He hopes to extract people's brains and set them up on their own in a situation of increased comfort and dignity, rendering them 'ecstatic by arranging for suitable patterns of electric current in selected regions of the brainstem.' He warns us only that 'a major problem may be the selection of lucky winners from the many who volunteer for disembodiment because of their wish to achieve a happier state of existence than that which is available to them by ordinary means.'[5]

Anyone browsing through shelves of science fiction and popular science can find plenty of similar neo-Cartesian fancies, expressed in a horrified distaste for the ordinary unmodified human body which one would normally expect only from someone like Tertullian or St Simeon Stylites. I owe this particular specimen, however, to Brian Easlea, who cites it in his excellent book *Science and Sexual Oppression*[6], where he also supplies some startling quotations from an apparently very different kind of writer: Sartre.

In his exaltation of the will, Sartre also has occasion to disown and denounce physical matter as alien to it, and therefore to our essential being. He describes the material world as 'viscous', clinging to us so as to entrap us. The drama appears in *Being and Nothingness* as follows:

> The For-Itself is suddenly *compromised*. I open my hands, I want to let go of the slimy and it sticks to me, it draws me, it sucks at me . . . It is a soft, yielding action, a moist and feminine sucking . . . it draws me to it as the bottom of a precipice might draw me . . . Slime is the revenge of the In-Itself. A

81

sickly-sweet, feminine revenge . . . The obscenity of the feminine sex is that of everything which 'gapes open.' It is *an
appeal to being*, as all holes are . . . Beyond any doubt her sex
is a mouth and a voracious mouth which devours the penis.[7]

I deliberately pick these bizarre instances of this isolation of the mind
and will because we have become so used to the greyer, more moderate forms that they pervade our thinking and are hard to notice. Of
course the cult of the cerebral has milder, less dangerous aspects.
Of course when it was (for perfectly sensible reasons) originally
invented it did not require such aberrations. But it has begun to
hypertrophy, and today it does require them. The individual will and
intellect are exalted in a way which can make any interference with
them – even that of other features of the organism to which they
belong, still more that of other people – seem an outrage.

Moral solipsism is on offer. It is not just that rational choice is
exalted high above the emotions. It has also been sharply separated
from them, treated as the central, necessary part of personal identity,
while the emotions are a chance, peripheral, extraneous matter. This
analysis is not just inhumane, it is incoherent. Choice and thought
cannot be separated from feeling; they are all aspects of a single
process. Exalters of choice and of the intellect are not immune from
feeling; they are following one set of feelings rather than another
without noticing it.

FOR FEELINGS, SEE WOMEN

The weaknesses of the intellectualist and voluntarist positions have
been often pointed out, but it has proved surprisingly hard to shift
them. What I want to say now is that this difficulty really does have
something to do with the fact that nobody applied them to women.
Both actual women and their symbolism were expected to remain
outside the blaze of cerebral daylight.

It was taken for granted that emotion would not actually lose its
influence, because women would still supply it. Families would still
be kept going. And the inconvenience caused by collisions between
so many hard, resistant, autonomous individuals would be kept
within bounds, because the customary cushions would still abound.
Hinc illae lacrimae.

Hence, that is, the alarm and horror which arose whenever it was
suggested that women too might have an intellect and a will. For
increasingly, as the cerebral view of personal identity developed, this

meant that they would each simply *be* an intellect and a will. All the other aspects of human nature, which had been left by a tacit division of labour entirely in their keeping, would be lost for ever.

This belief was shown repeatedly and with extraordinary naivety about the suffrage. When British women finally did vote, their political effect was slight and if anything conservative – they may well have been responsible for throwing out the Liberal government which had enfranchised them. But in advance the change seemed to many people, including many women, monstrously destructive and unthinkable.

PROMOTING CHOICE

This surely was because the vote was itself a central symbol of rationality. In voting, a man was conceived to operate as an abstraction – a coldly calculating citizen, who on many theories might be expected to be purely self-interested; an economic man. Social-contract mythology presented him as originally a bargainer who was quite free not to make any particular bargain, a shopper who might well go elsewhere. He might, as Rousseau instructs Émile to do when his education is completed, travel all over Europe with a view to asking himself: 'Which is my country?'

Rousseau completes this story by adding that one owes something to the land where one was born, and sending Émile home to his Sophie. But the social-contract formula contains also another possibility – the germ of a development towards a total and inhuman detachment, an unmitigated solipsistic egoism.

The way in which it has grown since Rousseau's day, especially in economic theory, has taken it steadily in this direction. The tacit refusal to extend it to women, a refusal which for some time concealed and partly mitigated its dangers and absurdities, can no longer be maintained, because feminists have rumbled it.

The choice now is between promoting everybody, equally, to the position of a Hobbesian or Sartrean solitary individual, or re-thinking the notion of individuality radically from scratch. It is cheering to see that feminists are at present proving extremely critical of the moves towards the first alternative, which were very common a decade or two back. They now seem likely to play their part in bringing about the second.

7

FREEDOM, FEMINISM AND WAR

—— •◆• ——

THE WAY in which feminism has developed has made some difficulties for this enterprise of rethinking individualism. Recently a young Nigerian feminist, who had been living in the West, wrote an article describing the difficulties she met with in returning to her native country. She found it painfully hard, she said, to put forward anything as essentially egoistic as Western feminism in the context of Nigerian life, where it was taken as a matter of course that all benefits would be shared. This remark impressed me, because it seemed to crystallize two very important conflicts. There is the conflict of values which arises between discordant elements within feminism itself. There is also the clash of priorities which arises when we try to relate feminism as a whole to other causes and ideals.

The internal conflict is by now very obvious and troublesome. On the one hand, feminism involves the assertion of women's individual rights as equal to those of men. This is a move which accepts and uses the strong individualism of the West, but just extends it to a larger public. It calls the bluff of the very odd lop-sided attitude which has prevailed since the eighteenth century, Rousseau's attitude, an attitude which treated all men as free and equal competitors in the social struggle, but expected the women to remain passively attached to them as unfree and unequal assistants.

On the new proposal, this competitive game stays the same, the only change is that there are now no assistants and the number of players is doubled. We might call this 'competitive feminism'. But it operates alongside a much deeper and wider feminist criticism of the game itself. There, women object altogether to the current Western obsession with competition and war. They point out that these are especially male preoccupations, and they suggest that the balance of ideals in our civilization has gone wrong. The more co-operative and friendly elements in life have been needlessly suppressed and for-gotten. This could be called 'co-operative feminism'. That is not an adequate name for it, because it is directly concerned with finding the right ends, not only with co-operation over means. But since the ends it looks to are ones which are likely to be achieved by co-operation and wrecked by competition, perhaps the name will do for now.

In feminist thought today, the clash between these two attitudes is serious. I don't at all think that it is unresolvable, that no unifying notion of feminism can be rescued from it. But this certainly has not been properly done yet, so it urgently calls for attention. It needs a lot of thought. And unluckily some feminists, early on in the current movement, objected to thought itself on principle, as a male institu-tion. This has caused a bit of confusion. The two attitudes are easily blurred together by the easy game of blaming men, an occupation which up to a point fits in quite well with both of them. Men can be blamed *either* for keeping women out of their world, *or* for making a world which no sensible woman would want to enter. But they cannot be effectively blamed for both at the same time.

Another trouble about blame is that, even where it is entirely appropriate and even necessary, it is inclined to be a barren, counter-productive proceeding. Blaming is an addictive habit and addiction to it is depressingly bad for the character. No doubt it serves to soothe cognitive dissonance, as other rousing group activities do. But we do not want just to soothe that dissonance. We want to sort out the issues which underlie it.

QUESTIONS OF PRIORITY

The need for a real resolution of the issues becomes still clearer when we turn to the other conflict, the external one of priorities. How can we relate the feminist endeavour to the other vast needs of our time, to the huge complex of problems which includes world hunger, the arms race and the destruction of the biosphere? Now it is not hard to see a place for co-operative feminism here because the competitive spirit is itself a central source of these disasters. On a world scale, the habit of competition can now no longer be seen as something primarily creative and productive. When resources grow short, it always becomes destructive. That is what is now happening all over the world, and it is only in the most cushioned parts of it that this can fail to be obvious.

We are brought up to associate competition with freedom, and indeed our whole notion of political freedom is at present coloured by this sporting metaphor. It tends to be seen as freedom to enter the game, to compete on equal terms against others, and of course to win . . . But the equal terms always apply to a limited public. They don't extend to the bulk of those who in the end are going to lose. They do not reach the South American Indians, or their forest, or even the unemployed in Western countries. This kind of freedom, if it is not checked by other ideals, begins to merge into the freedom of oppressors to oppress. Freedoms clash, which only shows how careful you have to be to know just what you mean by freedom.

It ought surely to be possible for co-operative feminism to criticize this barren, inadequate competitive ideal – to point out how its domination distorts all our other ideals, including its own favourite notions of freedom and equality – and to suggest more realistic ways of dealing with the conflicts of interest which divide us. It ought to be possible, and to some extent it does happen, but it is turning out much harder than it looks. There are great psychological difficulties about introducing these criticisms as the special contribution of women.

This is not very surprising. If co-operative ideals really were the *exclusive* property of women – if they were simply alien to men – there would be no reason why men should accept them, any more than why we should accept some incomprehensible set of ideals handed out by missionaries from another planet.

That certainly is not the situation. We know, both from history and from studies of many cultures, that, in the immense, obsessive emphasis it places on competition, Western culture is exceptional. Other ways of life are possible, and men as well as women in these cultures live by very different ideals. Moreover, even in our own culture very many men in many ways express strong dissatisfaction with the way things are going. Women surely can, without the slightest loss of dignity, acknowledge their male colleagues who have protested against war and rapine, from the Buddha on through Christ and a hundred others such as Montaigne, Blake, Mill and Kropotkin to the present day. And it seems compatible with both sides of feminism to accept this partnership as testifying that, as would be expected, male and female nature have a great deal in common. All the same, the present state of the world makes clear that the existing protest is not strong enough. Can we somehow make up the deficit by simply throwing the weight of half the population into the co-operative scale?

THE DANGER OF TOURNAMENTS

Up to a point this really is a possible strategy. An increased confidence among women themselves in the ideals which are thought to come naturally to them can indeed be a most valuable tool of change. But if we are to use it effectively, it seems vital to grasp certain psychological difficulties. It is the chronic curse of a competitive society that every new movement in it is liable to be seen as just one more competitor. There is a malign selection for one-sidedness.

On all sides tournaments abound. New demands easily appear as attacks and overtures to ritual combat. It is very hard for them to be considered on their merits as suggestions for the advantage of all. The language of *rights*, which in such a society is naturally central to morals, is easily debased to express a brute warfare of rival claimants, whose interests are incompatible – a mere trial of strength to be settled by muscle-power. Accordingly, in so far as feminism simply looks like a new set of demands pushing the interest of a particular group, it is liable to produce the usual counter-attack and give rise to a new competitive game. To recommend a more co-operative spirit in world affairs as something characteristically female is liable not to be the best way to get it accepted.

I don't want to sound too depressed and cynical about this obstacle. People can get used to this sort of move, and its off-putting effect certainly need not be total. All the same, it is present, and, as I have suggested, not without some reason. Men who are to be moved by ideals do have to recognize them as ones they can share. It seems essential that the argument should not proceed *primarily* in terms of men v. women, but more directly about the ideals themselves. I think there are serious criticisms to be made of current Western moral ideas, criticisms which can be put in the first place in gender-free terms, but which do express the ideals central to co-operative feminism and are made much clearer and more forceful by its special contribution. I will go on to sketch what I mean by this in a moment. But a word is probably necessary first on the question of priorities.

IS THERE AN ABSOLUTE PRIORITY?

It will be plain that I am asking, 'What is the place of feminism in resistance to militarism, to world hunger and to attacks on the biosphere?', and not 'what is the place of anti-militarism or green campaigning in advancing the cause of women'. I am not putting feminism before these other big issues. The reason for this is the simple one that, if the other issues are not directly dealt with, we shall all soon be dead. Local injustices, even very serious ones, therefore seem to me to fall within this framework. On the big issues, I think that feminism is an *aspect* of the necessary strategy, and in a way an essential aspect, but I don't see that it could possibly be the whole answer.

There is a familiar problem here about the relation between good causes, a problem which accounts for a great deal of friction and mutual exasperation between honourable people, with corresponding aid and comfort to the forces of darkness. Since what needs doing is never simple, and always has many aspects, people have to specialize to some extent in particular projects and endeavours. But because this complexity is both alarming and confusing, there is a constant temptation for each set of them to become reductive and to claim that their own aspect is the only key one, that it somehow leads the way for all the others.

This temptation is especially strong over a cause like feminism which has long been bizarrely neglected, and is at last receiving some attention. It is certain to be true, in such a case, that it can supply the missing piece for quite a number of puzzles which have been giving ·trouble because it was forgotten. It may very often alter the shape of a problem in a way which makes quite new solutions possible. But that is something different from the absolute priority which would entitle it to lead all the rest.

That absolute priority is often claimed on causal grounds – by saying that it will be impossible to solve the other problems till a certain chosen one has been dealt with. Thus, Marxism in its simpler forms long held out for the Revolution as being the necessary precondition of every other good thing, and therefore as proving anybody to be frivolous who put forward the claims of other ideals meanwhile. Against this view, people have naturally replied that it was idle to expect effective revolution to be made by those who despised more general ideals like humanity, honesty and social justice. These protesters insisted on a place for the seriousness of immediate reform, and sometimes insisted that reforms in private life are needed before it is possible to undertake anything political.

When feminism claims primacy, it evidently does it in the spirit of this second protest. In spite of some lively schemes for direct feminist revolutions, like Shulamith Firestone's book, *The Dialectic of Sex*,[1] it usually approaches the political by way of the personal. Feminism points out that accepted injustices within a society blunt people's sensibilities and make them readier to accept outside iniquities as well. These accepted injustices must therefore be dealt with, before wider issues can be approached. Now there is much in this. I find it quite understandable that anyone who is, for instance, concerned in running a refuge for battered wives and children, or a rape crisis centre, soon gets the impression that they are here dealing with an abomination so outstanding that it holds the key to all others, and must be remedied before it will be the slightest use engaging in any other political cause. The reaction is natural, but, as the whole history of reforms and revolutions shows, it is misleading and it must not be indulged.

THINKING ONESELF INTO A CORNER

There is usually no way in which any such abomination can be tackled without changing a much wider background, and this is bound to mean working *with* people whose initial interests are in other evils and other sides of the problem. In particular, if concentrating on these particular evils means that it is considered impossible to work with men, this seems like a fairly complete abdication of any serious intention of producing change at all. The people whose attitudes need to be changed here are, by definition, men, and if they cannot be talked to – if it is only possible to preach to the converted – then the whole enterprise has to be abandoned. More deeply still, if indignation has made it temporarily impossible to distinguish between men who share one's own attitude and ones who oppose it – if indignation has dissolved into mere tribal hatred – then the realistic responses which are the basis of feminism have been eroded, and the war of stereotypes can have no useful outcome.

I am suggesting that it can't be right for feminism to appear as an isolated cause. I have just been querying the way of thinking which isolates it temporarily, by treating it as the one essential first step to other causes, the key which will later open their doors. There is of course a more dramatic and lasting kind of isolation which can be prescribed for it in full-scale separatism, where it is seen as a self-sufficient end for all time. I am really not too sure how seriously this is meant or how it should be understood. But it certainly seems to imply, as much as the mere temporary isolationism, that women ought not to interest themselves in any political issue not concerned with claiming their own rights. I do not see how that issue can be isolated in this way from others and from the whole nature of our society.

That very ambiguous tag, 'the personal is the political', seems to need careful watching here. Its first meaning is the familiar one that personal troubles do not stand alone, that they can stem from wider institutions which need altering. Of course that is right. But it can also have the more ambitious sense that 'the political is *only* the personal' – that is, that we need not attend to any larger social issues except the ones which impinge on our own private lives. And this cannot be right. Political thinking, once started, is indivisible. And in fact this seclusion has not really been attempted. From the start of modern feminism, issues of race were treated as relevant to it, and this has usefully mitigated its narrowness. But our thought cannot stop there. Issues of peace and war have also often been seen as relevant. They surely are so, but I think our understanding of that relevance needs to be much clearer. The issue of what we mean by freedom is relevant too, and it has had much less attention. I will move on to that now.

THE FREEDOM OF SOLITUDE

There exists a notion of freedom in modern thought which treats it as total isolation, independence from all personal ties. Stemming from Nietzsche, and strongly supported by Sartre, this idea is much more respectfully treated than the more commonplace commercial ideal of free competition which I have already mentioned. Cut-throat competition in the market does have its disparaging critics. The lofty personal isolation of the Sartrian hero tends to get a much better press from intellectuals, even if it may in fact just as often lead to the cutting of throats. Obviously, this ideal does rest on an appeal to some important virtues – courage, honesty, active independence of mind.

Since the eighteenth century, the idea of these virtues in private life has been steadily developed as a destructive idea of cutting personal ties. It has appeared as an attack on domestic tyranny – in the first place, an attack on parental authority. The Oedipal drama, which in public politics meant overthrowing the monarchies, meant in private life that a young man would leave home, refusing the career which his father had prepared for him, and choose a life for himself. Countless novels have told this story, in which, for girls, resistance to a forced marriage plays the same part. Novels, even when they were officially very far from countenancing total disobedience, had a crucial role in this debunking of the concept of parental authority. The idea has been deeply woven into the imaginative picture of life set up by the Enlightenment. 'Authority', snorts Miss Howe in Richardson's *Clarissa* – 'what a full word is that in the mouth of a narrow-minded person who happens to have been born twenty years before one!'

At first, of course, these novels usually ended in marriage. But later, as the ideal of personal freedom expanded, marriage itself and all other close relationships were increasingly seen as oppressive. The only remaining possible happy ending – apart from death – was for the central character to be left alone, solitary, autonomous and rather bored, as he was in Samuel Butler's novel *The Way of All Flesh*. This Byronic pattern was of course at first developed only from the male point of view, and the snares to be escaped were seen as largely the snares of women. An active misogyny, stemming from Schopenhauer, colours many expressions of this myth, notably those of Nietzsche, Freud, Sartre and Bernard Shaw. It sometimes begins to seem doubtful whether we ought really to congratulate this hero on his courage in escaping from all personal ties, or to ask him why he was so exceptionally frightened of them in the first place.

It is not surprising, however, that women should have answered this myth by developing its mirror-image and issuing their own declaration of independence, asserting their determination to escape the snares of men, rather than wanting to ensnare them. This move was inevitable because it descends even more directly than the men's from the anti-authoritarianism of the Enlightenment. The authority of men over women was, after all, formal and officially recognized. It was clearly a remnant of the feudal, hierarchical way of thinking which had in theory been abandoned. To throw it off was simply to come in line with the official morality of the age. It was making real the idea of individual freedom, already widely accepted, which said that obligation ought to flow only from free choice. Each person should be linked to others only in so far as he or she personally chose. As moral philosophers were saying in the 1960s, the only real form of obligation is one's own voluntary promise.

THE PLACE OF CHOICE

Unfortunately, it doesn't take a lot of experience to discover that human life doesn't work like that. Even *a priori* indeed, the story is hardly convincing, because a tie or bond has two ends and both ends may not want to let go of it simultaneously. But beyond this, choice cannot in fact play more than a minor part in determining our obligations, if we want to live with other people at all. We do not choose our children, any more than we choose our parents, or our brothers and sisters. Only if we are amazingly rich or lucky can we choose our neighbours and those we work with.

Even when we do choose them, we can't guarantee that they will go on being as we want them to be or that they will go on choosing us. In general, even where choices are made, people cannot foresee, when they make them, all that they will later involve, because life is changeable and bonds are lasting. This notion of freedom, carried through consistently, would leave one alone, with a painfully narrow and solitary life, perhaps living scrupulously like Nietzsche, perhaps less so, like Howard Hughes.

Obviously, the ideal is not meant to be carried through consistently. Like a great deal of romantic thinking, it is designed primarily for the young, and especially at the moment when they need to leave home. At that time they can, if they are especially lucky, sit behind John Rawls's veil of ignorance and choose their society, saying, like Rousseau's Émile, 'I will travel to see which is my country'.[2] But this situation is rare. Even where it exists, its value is surely dynamic, as a means to a better context and the ties which will go with it. As a static, permanent ideal for *adults*, this deliberate critical isolation would be perverse and death-directed. Though it is often thought of as especially mature, it can as easily be seen as essentially adolescent and transitory. For a human life, people normally need to accept some society and to live within it.

I do not want to oversimplify this point. But I do think it is important that we should recognize that this exaltation of independence is an extremely strange feature of Western civilization, one which has its price and which often startles outsiders. It is not self-evidently the only right one. Plainly it is what the Nigerian writer I mentioned meant by the egoistic element in Western feminism. People who identify themselves deeply and habitually with their families and others around them find things like the attack on 'the family' – as such – deeply mystifying.

THE COMPLEXITY OF AIMS

Faced with this kind of criticism, Westerners tend to oscillate between conceding the point and muttering disapprovingly that these people are *unreconstructed* – they don't understand their own business. They don't know how to be happy . . . But the suggestion that we have a right to reconstruct others to our own blueprint is an alarming one. Of course this problem arises, not only in Africa, but in the West too. Many women consider that they are content to be domestic and absorbed in their families. Accordingly, a great deal of feminist endeavour is devoted to consciousness-raising – to persuading them that they are less contented than they think or that, if they actually are contented, then they ought not to be.

Now quite a lot of this is undoubtedly in order. People do waste their lives, and they are often glad to be helped in doing something about it. But I think it is very important that the positive aim – the ideal which inspires the process – should be clearly identified. If it is primarily independence, autonomy, 'authenticity', then there are quite narrow limits to its value. The natural state of human life is not total independence, which is a chimaera, but a balanced mutual dependence adjusted to people's needs. There is no point in women's exhausting themselves in trying to outdo men at the currently fashionable Western games of cut-throat business competition and death from thrombosis at forty, on the one hand, or of drinking alone in a bed-sitter while writing a novel, on the other, in order to live up to an unreal ideal of independence. If, however, the aim is *not* independence but integration into the sisterhood instead of the family, then we are back with an organic way of life, and reasons have to be given for the choice of this particular coral reef to grow in. The half-truth which the ideal of autonomy conveyed still needs to be asserted. It is no better to lose one's independence of mind to the local women's group than to one's parents or one's husband.

I am saying – and I'm sorry if it sounds boring – that all the different ideals have to be kept in balance together, that there is no quick way through to dealing with the world's large problems simply by putting first the interests of women, even if we could justify this unequal treatment as a form of affirmative action. Those interests cannot in general be separated from the other interests around them in a way that would make possible effective action.

Is there however, as is often said, some special feature of women's subordination which makes it in a sense primary? Is it somehow *the* key element in the whole noxious tangle, the thread which needs to be pulled first if we want to unravel the mess? I think it is certainly prominent among the many threads which must be pulled, but I doubt if the claim to absolute primacy makes much sense. It is true that emotional distortions of private life provide the models for much atrocious public behaviour. For instance, those brought up to see their mothers and sisters ignored and discounted will find it especially easy to pass on that treatment to others. But if we try to weigh this cause against many others – for instance, against the abuse of children or the old, or the mere natural narrowness of human sympathies – it is hard to see how any sort of priority could be established, or indeed why it should be. All evils are complex and need to be attacked from many sides at once.

Moreover it seems very important that the kind of distortions in private life which we have in mind here never affect only one side. Men's role becomes distorted as well as women's. It is a real misfortune for them, too, to be brought up for a bad role. It is interesting that both transvestism and the demand for sex changes in Western culture are predominantly male matters. In spite of the many, still persisting, special troubles facing women, it seems that being a man is still a narrower role, and in some ways a more frustrating one. Both roles need to be changed together. And since this cannot possibly be done without general consent, the project has to be presented in terms which make sense to both sexes. Women need a language that they can use to their sons as well as to their sisters.

If we want to free our thoughts from their deadlock – if we want to exchange and put together the fragments of the truth which we are all holding – we shall need to develop, on both sides, much more varied and imaginative ways of thinking, ones which do not limit us to preaching only to the converted. Feminist ideas can surely play a very important part in this, provided that they are kept free of a certain lethal kind of narrowness, which in any case is alien to the true core of feminism.

8

THE END OF ANTHROPOCENTRISM?

WHAT IS IT TO BE CENTRAL?

SO FAR, we have been looking at a series of distorting patterns which egoistic narrowness has imposed on our thoughts about human affairs. It has also, however, affected our relations with non-human affairs, indeed, with the whole cosmos that we live in.

Are human beings in some sense central to that cosmos? It used to seem obvious that they were. It seems less obvious now. But the idea is still powerful in our thinking, and it may be worthwhile asking just what it has meant.

There is of course a minor point of view from which we really are central. For our own lives, our own species does provide the natural focus. Our starting-point, the angle from which we look at things, is bound to be our own region. In the same way, if we think about *self-centredness*, each of us does unavoidably see our own self as in some sense the centre of the world.

This parallel is surely helpful. In neither case can we spread our consciousness impartially over the whole scene. We do have powers of sympathy, but since we are finite beings, those powers are necessarily limited. We have no choice but to be especially interested in ourselves and those close to us. As Bishop Butler pointed out, this kind of priority is not necessarily a bad thing. Indeed it's vital that we do love and care for ourselves properly. If we have not enough self-love, if we despise or hate ourselves, we cannot love other people. The trouble with human beings (he said) is not really that they love themselves too much; they ought to love themselves more. The trouble is simply that they don't love others enough.[1]

In that sense, then, the self *must* be the centre of each person's world and accordingly the word 'self-centred' seems at first to have had quite a good meaning. It was coined to describe the balanced state of heavenly bodies like the sun, spinning securely on their own

97

axes, rather than shooting off at an angle like badly-made tops. Figuratively, then, it was used to described well-organized, balanced people. Thus the Oxford English Dictionary quotes from a novel in 1895: 'He would be fixed at last, swinging steadily on a pivot of happiness . . . Now at last he would be self-centred'.

Interestingly, however, this image of independence early began to show a darker side. Thus the dictionary gives a remark by one Norris, writing *Practical Discourses* in 1693: 'The self-ending, self-centring man does in a very true sense idolize himself'. Again, it cites Dr Johnson's *Letters* (1783) – 'A stubborn sufficiency self-centred' – and Coleridge (1809): 'They pursue the interests of freedom steadily, but with narrow and self-centring views'. In short, the natural balance of the independent spinning top cannot be relied on for human social life. If there is too much ego in your cosmos, those around you are likely to go short. Charity may indeed begin at home, but it had better not end there.

This is now a commonly accepted moral principle, indeed, something of a platitude, not just for individual selves, but also for the various human groups into which they cluster – families, classes, professions, races, nations. Group chauvinism, as well as individual selfishness, is understood to be a serious fault. So far, indeed, we are on ground common to our whole moral tradition.

SPECIES POLITICS DURING THE ENLIGHTENMENT

If, however, we turn from self to species, things have not been so simple. Here people have seen themselves as placed, not just at the relative centre of a particular life, but at the absolute, objective centre of everything. The centrality of Man (*sic*) has been pretty steadily conceived, both in the West and in many other traditions, not as an illusion of perspective imposed by our starting-point, but as an objective fact, and indeed an essential fact, about the whole universe.

Christian thought grounded this status firmly on creation by a humanoid God who had made man in his (*sic*) own image in order to mark a quite special status among the ruck of ordinary, non-Godlike creatures. But this Christian account has not stood alone. Enlightenment thinkers who reckoned to be emancipated from such imagery were no less confident on the matter. Thus Kant: 'As the single being upon earth that possesses understanding, he [Man] is certainly titular lord of nature and, supposing that we regard nature as a teleological system, he is born to be its ultimate end.'[2]

Kant states here three themes which often recur and need a great deal of attention: the claim to dominance, the emphasis on intellect as its ground, and the reference to cosmic teleology. As for dominance, man is 'titular lord'. For beings who think hierarchically, this is no doubt a natural way to interpret centrality. What is alarming about it, however, is how easily the imagery of dominance escalates to that of exploitation and even warfare.

Thus Marx[3] observed that Capitalism had been right to reject 'the deification of nature ... thus nature becomes for the first time simply an object for mankind, purely a matter of utility'. More sharply still, Freud suggested that the right way to sublimate human aggression was to direct it away from other people and against the rest of the biosphere, 'combining with the rest of the human community and taking up the attack on nature, thus forcing it to obey human will, under the guidance of science'.[4] William James proposed the same solution to that problem in his famous essay on 'The Moral Equivalent of War'. In fact, the idea that human beings should use the intellectual power of science to conquer nature by war or suppression seems to have looked perfectly normal to many thinkers, at least up till the middle of this century, both in the capitalist world, and, if anything, still more so in the communist one. Thus John Passmore quotes (along with many other fascinating examples) M.N. Pokrovsky, writing in a *Brief History of Russia* in 1931:

> It is easy to foresee that in the future, when science and technique have attained to a perfection which we are as yet unable to visualize, nature will become soft wax in man's hands, which he will be able to cast into whatever form he chooses.[5]

DOUBT SEEPS IN

We can understand how people had reached this curious view. Starting from the already ambitious biblical position, human beings had for some centuries been performing many increasingly dazzling technological and scientific feats. At the same time, and partly as a result of these changes, various doctrines of historical progress had been developed, focusing attention still more strongly on the rising curve of human achievement, glorifying humans yet further, and making the gap between them and the rest of the biosphere look still wider.

At this same time, however, a whole string of potent intellectual developments were moving thought away from this cheerful pattern. The effect has been to leave that pattern now strangely isolated and conceptually unsupported, though still emotionally very strong. I think that a sizeable part of our present confusion may flow from our sense of anomaly here – from the Gestalt-shift between a wildly exaggerated, euphoric idea of human standing and a despairing nihilism about it which may be equally wild ('People are pollution'). Today, though we still often hear very flattering accounts of ourselves, we just as often come across much less flattering ones, and on the whole these are pronounced with more conviction.

Thus, early in this century William James (1904) remarked that 'man, biologically considered, and whatever else he may be into the bargain, is simply the most formidable of all the beasts of prey, and, indeed, the only one that preys systematically on its own species'. Or again, Arthur Koestler observed that 'The most persistent sound that reverberates through man's history is the beating of war-drums . . . Man can leave the earth and land on the moon, but cannot cross from East to West Berlin. Prometheus reaches for the stars with an insane grin on his face and a totem-symbol in his hand.'[6]

Of course dark remarks of this sort are not new. There was always an ambivalence within Christian thought that called for humility and penitence and reminded us that our righteousness was as filthy rags. But certain changes in the modern age have given this kind of thinking so much more force that they might, at a glance, be seen as heralding the end of anthropocentrism.

THE PARADOX OF SCIENCE

What, then, have been these eroding changes? In the first place, of course, scientific progress itself began to cast doubts on the whole euphoric way of thinking. The universe has turned out to be both so much larger and so much less tidily organized than it used to seem that the idea of its having any centre, in a literal physical sense, no longer makes much sense. And though we might think that it should be easy to accept these new factual beliefs without losing what the older ones used to symbolize, it turns out that this imagery is in fact quite hard to shift. Symbols that persist in this way, when beliefs about the facts have changed, always deserve our attention.

Several different sciences have converged to alarm us here. Astronomy now tells us that there is no physical centre and no absolute up and down. There surrounds us, instead, a formless stage so vast, both in time and space, that even the most splendid human actors are almost imperceptible as they move upon it – insects or bacteria, at best. Biology adds that, even among the living things which have lately entered on this scene, human beings are particularly late and perhaps accidental arrivals. Their shape, too, does not appear to be so much a direct imprint from God as a slight variation on an existing primate pattern. Xenophanes, in fact, was right: if horses and cattle had gods, they would make them in the shape of horses and cattle. Man has made God in his own image.

Geography adds that the continents which we have usually thought of as at least a firm grounding for our part of the stage are themselves on the move. Most recently, too, ecology has told us that we are by no means securely moulding wax-like nature to suit our needs and are never likely to do so. On the contrary, we are busily sawing off the branches we sit on, and can only cease to do that if we attend respectfully to the internal guiding principles of nature instead of trying to distort it through ones invented by ourselves.

More widely still, however, there is a metaphysical change in the scientific perspective. The teleological assumptions that seemed to hold the symbolic core of 'anthropocentrism' in place are themselves no longer deemed scientific. The idea of a central cosmic purpose is as foreign to modern science as the idea of a central location is. The word 'anthropocentric' itself seems to have been invented to make just this point. Thus the Oxford Dictionary quotes Haeckel (or his translator into English) writing in 1876 of 'the anthropocentric error, that man is the premeditated aim of the creation of the earth'.

The paradox here – comic or tragic, as you choose to look at it – is that science, which has always seemed a particularly bright jewel in the crown of the titular lord, turns out also, paradoxically, to be an axe cutting away the floor under his throne. Nor is science alone in this destructive work; political theory plays an equally double part. After the Enlightenment, what are we doing with the notion of a titular lord anyway? If we are proud of science, we are surely still more proud of discovering that government should always be by consent. Its authority comes from below, from those who accept it, not from an outside ruler, as in the Divine Right of Kings. The idea of being a lord arbitrarily appointed from outside, more particularly a violent lord, liable at the drop of a hat to make war on his disobedient subjects, doesn't suit our self-image at all. Yet, if we keep the traditional reasoning and imagery, that is how we are supposed to see ourselves.

101

ANTHROPIC ESCAPISM

What is to be done about all this? It is quite interesting that some desperate efforts have been made to extend modern science so as to make it endorse the traditional picture, most strikingly through the Strong Anthropic Principle. This rules that 'The Universe must have those properties which allow life to develop within it at some stage in its history'.[7] This is considered necessary because matter cannot really function unless it is observed, and observed in the special way in which physicists observe quantum events. (A confused memory of Berkeleyan idealism is evidently at work here.) Human perception, and indeed the perception of contemporary scientists, is thus absolutely indispensable to the existence of the cosmos. The logic of this approach appears to be more or less that of the old limerick:

> There once was a man who said, 'God
> Must find it exceedingly odd
> If he finds that this tree
> Continues to be
> When there's no-one about in the quad.'

Officially, this quasi-idealist approach is not supposed to imply that the cosmos works with the aim of producing the observer who will save it. But it is usually combined with the thought that the constitution of the existing universe is so extraordinarily improbable that the fact of its development can only be accounted for by the need to produce just one of its existing artefacts. And by a remarkable coincidence, this selected artefact turns out not to be a set of giraffes or redwood trees or colonial jellyfish, but the species Homo Sapiens – especially, of course, in its current manifestation as Homo Sapiens Physicus.

In effect, this can only be an attempt to bring back teleology – to renew the notion of a cosmic drama with a central role for Man, not in the context of religion, nor with any explicitly defended philosophical assumptions, but nominally as a simple, objective part of physics. This principle teaches that the universe has indeed had the production of Man as its central business, but that Man is needed simply to do physics, to collapse certain wave-functions by observing quantum events, and thereby to make the universe itself at last fully and properly real.

Until then it was not thus real, for, as John Wheeler explains, 'Acts of observer-participancy – via the mechanism of the delayed-choice experiment – in turn give tangible "reality" to the universe not only now but back to the beginning'.[8] Professors Barrow and Tipler add that Man, having performed this feat, will then proceed to computerize himself and to occupy the whole of space by colonization, arriving finally at the Omega Point in possession of all the information that there is, and thereby in some sense apparently becoming God. (Their most startling claims about this may be found at the end of their book, and especially in its concluding sentences.)

I have discussed this amazing project elsewhere,[9] and we will return to it briefly in Chapter 11. The point that is relevant here is that this sort of thing is in no sense science. It is simply a piece of wild metaphysics, made possible by the weird metaphorical language already in use on the topics of quantum mechanics, time and probability theory. Ignorance about how metaphors work is widespread among modern English-speaking physicists, and is particularly deep among British ones. They very much need to read the chapter on Science in Janet Martin Soskice's sharp little book *Metaphor and Religious Language*,[10] and also Graham Richards's *On Psychological Language*.[11]

WHY ALL OR NOTHING?

What matters here, however, is not the muddles but the point of the suggestion. The Anthropic Principle seems aimed, somewhat desperately, at bridging the gap just mentioned – the gap that yawns in our current thinking between our immense sense of our own importance on the local scene and our apparent total insignificance in the objective universe.

We cannot bridge that gap if we insist on an all-or-nothing solution. The anthropicists are making a desperate effort to keep *all*. They are in fact setting up far the highest claims ever made for the importance of our species, because they do not even have the background figure of God to moderate our status.

While God is present, Man can be reduced to the figure of a responsible steward, even if he remains, in some sense, central among earthly creatures. But for the anthropicists, Man replaces God as creator, not just of earth, but of everything. In effect, they are offering us anthropolatry. As Norris put it, 'The self-ending, self-centring man does in a very true sense idolize himself'.

I suggest that the reason why cosmologists do this is not necessarily that they are more conceited than the rest of us, but that the fear of total insignificance produces a violent reaction, leading people to claim immense, inconceivable kinds of significance. Exactly as happens over individual paranoia, frightened subjects react against being down-graded by grading themselves up – if necessary, indefinitely, and so becoming gods. The trouble starts, surely, with the fact that, when our traditional symbols are attacked, we do not stop thinking symbolically, we just change the drama that surrounds the symbol.

When the cosmic stage on which we used to figure becomes larger, we do not drop the idea of any such stage. Instead, we see ourselves as shrinking puppets, and eventually as ants or bacteria, still performing on this same expanding stage . . . Because this is unbearable, people look for a counter-symbol, a story which can somehow be taken as scientifically literal, and which yet gives us back our key part in the drama.

What we need to do instead, I suggest, is to change the symbolism in a deeper and more discriminating way. We never needed that vast cosmic stage in the first place, and only very lately have we had it. Our business has never been with anything outside our own planet.

We do indeed need a sense of destiny – a sense of a larger background, a context within which our own lives make sense. We need the idea of a drama in which we are acting. We have to have a sense of the sort of role that is expected of us. We need that sense whether or no we believe in God, whether or no we are important and influential people, whether or no we understand where it comes from.

All cultures supply this sort of background framework – indeed, doing so is one of their most basic functions. We need it both for ourselves individually and for all the groups with which we seriously identify. That is what it is for life to have a meaning. But nothing fixes in advance the range of beings that must figure in our drama. Nothing forces us to take the vast extra-terrestrial background into our theatre. And certainly nothing commits us to swallowing or conquering all figures in the drama who are outside our own group.

At every level – both for the individual and for various kinds of group – there is a temptation to supply this drama simply by drawing a firm line between ourselves and a range of opponents. That is always the easiest way to give life a meaning. Individuals can set themselves against the whole world; Ajax defies the lightning. Similarly group members can set their group against everybody outside it, and life so organized can go on charmingly for the inside circle. All disasters, even death, are more easily faced in this pugnacious context which so readily gets the adrenalin flowing. This is the tendency which has again and again fixed people in mutually destructive, confrontational groups. It is surely the one that has accounted for the exclusive, pugnacious glorification of our own species in earlier thinking.

WHAT SHOULD WE CALL IT?

I do not think Anthropocentrism is the best name for this habit. It is, no doubt, a word that can be used at the everyday level, and at that level I am not trying to get rid of it. But if we try to put much weight on it, it can lead us into trouble. In the first place, as I said at the outset, there is a sense in which it is right for us to feel that we are the centre of our own lives. Attempts to get rid of that sense would be doomed in the same way as Stoical attempts to tell people not to care especially about themselves, or about those dear to them. As Bishop Butler (again) pointed out in his Sermon on Compassion (Section 11), puritanism of this sort can only be destructive. It may succeed in damaging the particular affections it attacks, but it has no power to produce nobler, more universal affections to replace them. And in controversy, such unrealistic puritanism is always damaging to one's own cause.

We need, then, to recognize that people do right, not wrong, to have a particular regard for their own kind and their own species. From a practical angle, this recognition does not harm green causes, because the measures needed today to save the human race are, by and large, the same measures that are needed to save the rest of the biosphere. There simply is no lifeboat option by which human beings can save themselves alone, either as a whole or in particular areas. If there were, this issue of emotional centrality might be a serious one, but there isn't. There are indeed local conflicts of interests over things like culling. But in general, in the kind of major emergency we have at present, the interests of different species coincide so widely that really enlightened self-interest would not dictate seriously different policies from species-altruism. I don't, therefore, see any need to dispute about the use of the word 'anthropocentrism' in this very limited sense.

When, however, we leave that intelligible ground – when 'anthropocentrism' is taken to mean an absolute claim to be at the centre of the universe – I simply do not know what this metaphor is supposed to mean at all. The Anthropicists are probably doing us a service by sketching out a possible meaning for it, since that meaning is so ludicrous as to reduce the whole idea to absurdity. What is commonly *meant* by the word 'anthropocentric' today, however, is something much more ordinary and much less intellectually ambitious. It is simple human chauvinism, narrowness of sympathy, comparable to national or race- or gender-chauvinism. It could also be called *exclusive humanism*, as opposed to the hospitable, friendly, inclusive kind.

105

That chauvinism is surely as indefensible rationally as the chauvinism of smaller human groups. Enlightenment thinking has certainly built protective barriers round it by devices like defining the idea of 'rights' in a way that confines it to articulate humans who can speak in law-courts, and ruling that these rights can only belong to those who have, in a recognized human sense, duties. These constructions seem to me evidently artificial and unconvincing once the spotlight of attention actually reaches them. (I have discussed them myself elsewhere.)[12] As tools of admirable campaigning for the Rights of Man, these ideas were originally aimed at extending concern to the whole human race, not at shutting it off from dogs and horses. Some of the major Enlightenment sages, such as Tom Paine, Montaigne and Voltaire, were in fact much concerned about the sufferings of animals, and Bentham surely spoke for the deeper spirit of Enlightenment humanitarianism when he said, 'The question is not, Can they talk? Nor, Can they reason? But: Can they suffer?'

Certainly this wider perspective leaves us with some hard problems. We have to arbitrate all sorts of local inter-species conflicts; we do not have a tidy system of Rights and Duties that will always tell us how to do so. But then, did anybody ever suppose that we did have one, even on the human scene? Such a project would be still less plausible if it were applied, as human chauvinists might still like to apply it, to all conflicts of interests between species in the fast-changing, distracted world that we have today.

The kind of anthropolatry that would always set immediate human interests above those of other life-forms is surely no longer defensible. The strong contributions from egoism, which were incorporated into Enlightenment individualism, did have uses in their own day. But today we need less, not more, ego in our cosmos, both individually and collectively. Our next business is somehow to forge the ways of thinking that will help us to move in this direction. In the next chapter, we will look at some confusions which sharply light up the need for that move.

9

IS A DOLPHIN A PERSON?

THE UNDOUBTING JUDGE

THIS QUESTION came up during the trial of the two people who, in May 1977, set free two bottle-nosed dolphins used for experimental purposes by the University of Hawaii's Institute of Marine Biology. It is an interesting question for a number of reasons, and I want to use most of this discussion in interpreting it, and tracing its connexion with several others which may already be of concern to us. I shall not go into details of the actual case, but shall rely on the very clear and thoughtful account which Gavin Daws gives in his paper, '"Animal Liberation" as Crime'.[1]

Kenneth le Vasseur, the first of the two men to be tried, attempted through his counsel what is called a 'choice of evils' defence. In principle the law allows this in cases where an act, otherwise objectionable, is necessary to avoid a greater evil. For this defence to succeed, the act has to be (as far as the defendant knows) the only way of avoiding an imminent, and more serious, harm or evil to himself or to 'another'.

Le Vasseur, who had been involved in the care of the dolphins, believed that their captivity, with the conditions then prevailing in it, actually endangered their lives. His counsel,

> in his opening statement for the defence, spoke of the exceptional nature of dolphins as animals; bad and rapidly deteriorating physical conditions at the laboratory; a punishing regimen for the dolphins, involving overwork, reductions in their food rations, the total isolation they endured, deprived of the company of other dolphins, even of contact with humans in the tank, deprived of all toys which they had formerly enjoyed playing with – to the point where Puka, having refused to take part consistently in experimental sessions, developed

self-destructive behaviours symptomatic of deep disturbance, and finally became lethargic – 'comatose.' Le Vasseur, seeing this, fearing that death would be the outcome, and knowing that there was no law that he could turn to, believed himself authorized, in the interests of the dolphins' well-being, to release them. The release was not a theft in that Le Vasseur did not intend to gain anything for himself. It was intended to highlight conditions in the laboratory.

(Daws: 356–67)

But was a dolphin 'another'? The judge thought not. He said that 'another' would have to be another person, and he defined dolphins as property, not as persons, as a matter of law. A dolphin could not be 'another person' under the penal code. The defence tried and failed to get the judge disqualified for prejudice. It then asked leave to go to Federal Court in order to claim that Thirteenth Amendment rights in respect of involuntary servitude might be extended to dolphins. This plea the judge rejected:

> Judge Doi said, 'We get to dolphins, we get to orangutans, chimpanzees, dogs, cats. I don't know at what level you say intelligence is insufficient to have that animal or thing, or whatever you want to call it, a human being under the penal code. I'm saying that they're not under the penal code and that's my answer.'
>
> (Daws: 365)

At this point – which determined the whole outcome of the trial – something seemed perfectly obvious to the judge about the meaning of the words 'other' and 'person'. What was it? And how obvious is it to everybody else? In the answer just given, he raises the possibility that it might be a matter of intelligence, but he rejects it. That consideration, he says, is not needed. The question is quite a simple one; no tests are called for. The word 'person' just means a human being.

WHAT ARE PERSONS?

I think that this is a very natural view, but not actually a true one, and the complications which we find when we look into the use of this interesting word are instructive. In the first place, there are several well-established and indeed venerable precedents for calling non-human beings 'persons'.

108

One concerns the persons of the Trinity, and indeed the person-hood of God. Another is the case of 'legal persons' – corporate bodies such as cities or colleges, which count as persons for various purposes, such as sueing and being sued. As Blackstone says, these 'corporations or bodies politic . . . are formed and created by human laws for the purposes of society and government'; unlike 'natural persons', who can only be created by God. The law, then, can if it chooses create persons; it is not a mere passive recorder of their presence (as indeed Judge Doi implied in making his ruling a matter of law and not of fact). Thirdly, what may look nearer to the dolphins, the word is used by zoologists to describe the individual members of a compound or colonial organism, such a jellyfish or coral, each having (as the dictionary reasonably puts it) 'a more or less independent life'.[2]

There is nothing stretched or paradoxical about these uses, for the word does not in origin mean 'human being' or anything like it. It means a mask, and its basic general sense comes from the drama. The 'masks' in a play are the characters who appear in it. Thus, to quote the Oxford Dictionary again, after 'a mask', it means 'a character or personage acted, one who plays or performs any part, a character, relation or capacity in which one acts, a being having legal rights, a juridical person'.

The last two meanings throw a sharp light on the difference between this notion and that of being human. Not all human beings need be persons. The word *persona* in Latin does not apply to slaves, though it does apply to the State as a corporate person. Slaves have, so to speak, no speaking part in the drama; they do not figure in it; they are extras.

There are some entertaining similar examples about women. Thus:

One case, brought before the US Supreme Court in the 1890s, concerned Virginia's exclusion of a woman from the practice of the law, although the pertinent statute was worded in terms of 'persons'. The Court argued that it was indeed up to the State's Supreme Court '*to determine whether the word 'person' as used (in the Statute) is confined to males,* and whether women are admitted to practise law in that Commonwealth'. The issue of whether women must be understood as included by the word 'persons' continued even into the twentieth century . . . In a Massachusetts case in 1931 . . . women were denied eligibility for jury service, although the statute stated that every 'person qualified to vote' was so eligible. The Massachusetts Supreme Court asserted: 'No intention to include women can be deduced from the omission of the word male.'[3]

FINDING THE RIGHT DRAMA

What is going on here? We shall not understand it, I think, unless we grasp how deeply drama is interwoven with our thinking, how intimately its categories shape our ideas. People who talk like this have a clear notion of the drama which they think is going on around them. They know who is supposed to count in it and who is not. Attempts to introduce fresh characters irritate them. They are inclined to dismiss these attempts sharply as obviously absurd and paradoxical. The question who is and who is not a person seems at this point a quite simple and clear-cut one. Bertie Wooster simply is not a character in *Macbeth* and that is the end of the matter.

It is my main business here to point out that this attitude is too crude. The question is actually a very complex one, much more like 'who is important?' than 'who has got two legs?' If we asked 'who is important?' we would know that we needed to ask further questions, beginning with 'important for what?' Life does not contain just one purpose or one drama, but many interwoven ones. Different characters matter in different ways. Beings figure in some dramas who are absent from others, and we all play different parts in different scripts.

Even in ordinary human life, it is fatal to ignore this. To insist on reducing all relationships to those prescribed by a single drama – such, for instance, as the Social Contract – is disastrous. Intellectuals are prone to such errors, and need to watch out for them. But when we come to harder cases, where the variation is greater – cases such as abortion, euthanasia or the treatment of other species – this sort of mistake is still more paralysing. That is why these cases are so helpful in illuminating the more central ones.

It is clear that, over women, those who limited the use of the concept 'person' felt this difficulty. They did not want to deny altogether that women were persons, since in the dramas of private life women figured prominently. Public life, however, was a different stage, whose rules and conventions excluded them (queens apart) as completely as elephants or angels. The fact that private life often impinges on public was an informal matter and could not affect this ruling. Similarly at Rome, it is clear that slaves actually played a considerable part in life. In Greek and Roman comedy ingenious slaves, both male and female, often figure as central characters, organizing the intrigue and supplying the brains which the hero and heroine themselves unfortunately lack. This, however, was not going to get them legal rights. The boundaries of particular situations and institutions served to compartmentalize thought and to stop people raising questions about the rights and status of those who were for central purposes currently disregarded.

I think it will be helpful here to follow out a little further the accepted lines of usage for the word person. How complete is its link with the human bodily form? What, for instance, about intelligent alien beings? Could we call them persons? If not, then contact with them – which is certainly conceivable – would surely require us to coin a new word to do the quite subtle moral job which is done at present by 'person'. The idea of a person in the almost technical sense required by morality today is the one worked out by Kant.[4] It is the idea of a rational being, capable of choice and therefore endowed with dignity, worthy of respect, having rights; one that must be regarded always as an end in itself, not only as a means to the ends of others.

Because this definition deals solely with rational qualities, it makes no mention of human form or human descent, and the spirit behind it would certainly not license us to exclude intelligent aliens, any more than disembodied spirits. The moral implications of the word 'person' would therefore, on our current Kantian principles, surely still have to attach to whatever word we might coin to include aliens. C.S. Lewis, describing a planet where there are three distinct rational species, has them use the word *hnau* for the condition which they all share, and this term is naturally central to the morality of all of them.[5]

Now if intelligence is really so important to the issue, a certain vertigo descends when we ask 'where do we draw the line?' because intelligence is a matter of degree. Some inhabitants of our own planet, including whales and dolphins, have turned out to be a lot brighter than was once thought. Quite how bright they are is not yet really clear to us. Indeed it may never become so, because of the difference in the kind of brightness appropriate to beings with very different sorts of life. How can we deal; with such a situation?

ATTENDING TO THE MIDDLE GROUND

The first thing needed is undoubtedly to get away from the single, simple, black-and-white antithesis with which Kant started, the antithesis between persons and things. Most of Kant's argument is occupied with this, and while it remains so he does not need to make finer distinctions. *Things* (he says) can properly be used as means to human ends in a way in which *people* cannot. Things have no aims of their own; they are not subjects but objects.

111

Thing-treatment given to people is exploitation and oppression. It is an outrage, because, as Kant exclaims, 'a man is not a thing'. Masters sell slaves; rulers deceive and manipulate their subjects; employers treat their secretaries as part of the wallpaper. By dwelling on the simple, stark contrast involved here, Kant was able to make some splendid moral points which are still vital to us today, about the thorough-going respect which is due to every free and rational human being. But the harsh, bright light which he turned on these situations entirely obscured the intermediate cases. A mouse is not a thing either, before we even start to think about a dolphin.

I find it interesting that, just as the American courts could not quite bring themselves to say that women were not persons, so Kant cannot quite get around to saying what his theory certainly implies, that animals are things. He does say that they 'are not self-conscious and are there merely as a means to an end',[6] that end being ours. But he does not actually call them things, nor does he write off their interests. In fact he emphatically condemns cruel and mean treatment of them. But, like many other humane people who have got stuck with an inadequate moral theory, he gives ingeniously unconvincing reasons for this. He says – what has gone on being said ever since – that it is only because cruelty to animals may lead on to cruelty to humans, or degrade us, or be a sign of a bad moral character, that we have to avoid it.

This means that if we can show that, for instance, venting our ill-temper on the dog will prevent our doing it on our families, or if we can produce certificates to show that we are in general people of firm moral character, not easily degraded, we can go ahead with a clear conscience. Dog-bashing, properly managed, could count as a legitimate form of therapy, along with gardening, pottery and raffia-work. In no case would the physical materials involved be directly considered, because all equally would be only objects, not subject. And there is nothing degrading about simply hitting an objects.

In spite of the appalling cruelty which human beings show towards animals the world over, it does not seem likely that anyone regards them consistently in this light, as objects. Spasms of regard, tenderness, comradeship and even veneration, alternating with unthinking callousness, seem to make up the typical human attitude to them. And towards fellow-human-beings too, a rather similar alternation is often found. So this cannot really be an attitude confined to things. Actually even cruelty itself, when it is deliberate, seems to require that its objects should not be mere physical objects, but should be capable of minding what is done to them, of responding as separate characters in the drama.

More widely, the appeal of hunting, and also of sports such as bull-fighting, seems to depend on the sense of outwitting and defeating a conscious quarry or opponent, 'another', able to be one's opposite in the game or drama. The script distinctly requires non-human characters, who can play their parts well or badly. Moby Dick is not an extra. And the degradingness of deliberate cruelty itself surely requires this other-regarding element. 'Another' is not always another human being.

INDIRECT JUSTIFICATIONS

The degradingness of cruelty is of course widely admitted, and le Vasseur's counsel used this admission as the ground of an alternative defence. He drew attention to his client's status as a state employee, which conferred authority on him to act as he did in coming to the defence of 'another', in this case the United States, whose social values were injured by what was being done to the dolphins. This argument was rejected, on the ground that, in the eyes of the law, cruelty to animals is merely a misdemeanour, whereas theft is a felony. Accordingly the choice of evils could not properly be resolved in such a way as to make theft the less serious offence. It is interesting that this argument makes no objection to treating the United States as 'another' or 'another person' – it does not insist that a person simply means a human being – but rests instead on contending that this 'other' finds its values more seriously attacked by theft than by cruelty to dolphins.

This sort of argument is not easy to come to grips with, even in the case of an ordinary individual person, still less in that of a nation. How serious an evil is cruelty? Once it is conceded that the victim's point of view does not count, that the injury is only to the offender or some body of which he is part, we seem to be cut off from the key considerations of the argument and forced to conduct it in a strained manner, from grounds which are not really central. Is cruelty necessarily depraving? On this approach, that seems partly to be a factual question about how easily people are depraved, and partly perhaps an aesthetic one about how far cruel acts are necessarily disgusting and repellent.

These acts seem to be assimilated now to others which are repellent without being clearly immoral, such as eating the bodies of people whom one has not killed, or watching atrocities over which one has no control. The topic becomes a neighbour of pornography rather than of abortion and euthanasia. (In the disputes about permissiveness in the

1960s, an overlap actually developed here at times, as when a London art gallery organized a happening in which some fish were to be electrocuted as part of the show, and efforts to ban this were attacked as censorious manifestations of aesthetic narrow-mindedness.)

Something seems to have gone wrong with the thinking here. The distinctive feature of actions attacked on purely aesthetic grounds should surely be that their effects are confined to those who actually perform them. No other sentient being is harmed by them. That is why they pose problems for libertarians, when bystanders object to them. But cruelty does not pose this kind of problem, since the presence of 'another' who is harmed is essential to it. In our case it is the dolphin, who does seem to be 'another'. Can we avoid thinking of it in this way? Can the central objection to cruelty really be something rather indirect, such as its being in bad taste?

MORAL CHANGE AND THE LAW

The law seems to have ruled thus here. And in doing this, the law shows itself to be in a not uncommon difficulty, one that arises when public opinion is changing. Legal standards are not altogether independent of moral standards. They flow from them and crystallize in ways designed to express certain selected moral insights. When those insights change deeply enough, the law changes. But there are often jolts and discrepancies here, because the pace of change is different. New moral perceptions require the crystals to be broken up and reformed, and this process takes time. Changes of this kind have repeatedly altered the rules surrounding the central crux which concerns us here; the stark division of the world into persons and property. Changing attitudes to slavery are a central case, to which we must come back in a minute. But it is worth noticing first that plain factual discoveries too can make a difference.

When our civilization formed the views on the species barrier which it still largely holds, all the most highly-developed non-human animals were simply unknown. Legend apart, it was assumed that whales and dolphins were much like fish. The great apes were not even discovered till the eighteenth century and no real knowledge of their way of living was acquired until within the last few decades. About better-known creatures too, there was a very general ignorance and unthinking dismissal of available evidence; their sociality was not noticed or believed in. The central official intellectual tradition of our culture never expected to be forced to subtilize its crude, extreme, unshaded dichotomy between man and beast. In spite of the efforts of many concerned thinkers, from Plutarch to Montaigne and from Blake to John Stuart Mill, it did not develop other categories.

If alien beings landed tomorrow, lawyers, philosophers and social scientists would certainly have to do some very quick thinking. (I don't expect the aliens myself, but they are part of the imaginative furniture of our age, and it is legitimate to use them to rouse us from our dogmatic slumbers.) Science fiction, though sometimes helpful, has far too often side-tracked the problem by making its aliens just scientists with green antennae – beings whose 'intelligence' is of a kind to be instantly accepted at the Massachusetts Institute of Technology, only of course a little greater. Since neither dolphins nor gorillas write doctoral theses, this would still let us out as far as terrestrial non-human creatures were concerned. 'Persons' and their appropriate rights could still go on being defined in terms of this sort of intelligence, and we could quietly continue to poison the pigeons in the park any time that we felt like it.

The question is, why should this kind of intelligence be so important, and determine the limits of our moral concern? It is often assumed that we can only owe duties to beings capable of speech. Why this should be thought is not altogether clear. At a simple level, Bentham surely got it right: 'The question is not *can they talk*? Nor *can they reason*? But *can they suffer*?'.[7] With chimps, gorillas and dolphins, however, there is now a further problem, because people have been trying, apparently with some degree of success, to teach them certain kinds of language. This project might have taught us a great deal about just what new categories we need in our attempt to classify beings more subtly. But unluckily it has been largely obscured by furious opposition from people who still have just the two categories, and who see the whole proceeding as an illicit attempt to smuggle contraband from one to the other.

This reaction is extremely interesting. What is the threat? Articulate apes and cetaceans are scarcely likely to take over the government. What might happen, however, is that it would become much harder to exclude them from moral consideration. In particular, their use as experimental subjects might begin to look very different. Can the frontier be defended by a resolute and unbreakable refusal to admit that these animals can talk?

THE MEANING OF FELLOWSHIP

It is understandable that people have thought so, but this surely cannot really be the issue. What makes creatures our fellow-beings, entitled to basic consideration, is not intellectual capacity, but emotional fellowship. And if we ask what powers can give a higher claim, bringing some creatures nearer to the degree of consideration which is due to humans, what is most relevant seems to be sensibility, social and emotional complexity of the kind which is expressed by the forming of deep, subtle and lasting relationships. The gift of imitating certain intellectual skills which are important to humans is no doubt an indicator of this, but it cannot be central. We already know that both apes and dolphins have this kind of social and emotional complexity.

If we ask what elements in 'persons' are central in entitling them to moral consideration, we can, I think, get some light on the point by contrasting the claim of these sensitive social creatures with that of a computer of the present generation, programmed in a manner which entitles it, by current controversial usage, to be called 'intelligent' and certainly able to perform calculations impossible to human beings. That computer does not trouble our sleep with any moral claims, and would not do so however much more 'intelligent' it became, unless it eventually seemed to be conscious, sensitive and endowed with emotions.

If it did seem so, we should have the Frankenstein problem in an acute form. (The extraordinary eagerness with which Frankenstein drove his researches to this disastrous point is something which contemporary monster-makers might like to ponder.) But those who at present emphasize the intelligence of computers do not see any reason to want to call them persons, nor to allow for them as members of the moral community. Speech alone, then, would scarcely do this job for the apes. What is at issue is the already glaring fact, which speech would make it finally impossible to deny, that they mind what happens to them – that they are highly sensitive social beings.

These considerations are not, I think, ones confined to cranks or extremists. They seem fairly widespread today, and probably occur at times to all of us, however uncertain we may be what to do about them. If so, and if the law really allows them no possible weight, then we seem to have reached the situation where the law will have to be changed, because it shocks morality. There is an obvious precedent, to which the dolphin-liberators tried to appeal:

> When the dolphins were taken from the tanks, a message was left behind identifying the releasers as the 'Undersea Railroad', a reference to the Undeground Railroad, the Abolitionists' slave-freeing network of pre-Civil War days. Along the

Underground Railroad in the 1850s, it sometimes happened that juries refused to convict people charged with smuggling slaves to freedom. That was the kind of vindication le Vasseur and Sipman were looking for . . . They did not consider themselves to be criminals. In fact they took the view that, if there was a crime, it was the crime of keeping dolphins – intelligent, highly aware creatures with no criminal record of their own – in solitary confinement, in small, concrete tanks, made to do repetitious experiments, for life.

(Daws: 362)

If we go back to the alien beings for a moment and consider whether even the most intelligent of them would have the right to keep any visiting human beings, however stupid, in these conditions, even those of us least partial to astronauts may begin to see the point which le Vasseur and Sipman were making. It surely cannot be dismissed merely by entrenching the law round the definition of the word 'person'. We need new thinking, new concepts and new words, not (of course) just about animals but about our whole relation to the non-human world. We are not less capable of providing these than people were in the 1850s, so we should get on with it.

11

VISIONS: SECULAR, SACRED
AND SCIENTIFIC

WIDENING VIEWS

IN THE last three chapters, we have been considering relations between human beings and various parts of the wider, non-human world. This excursion beyond the human scene is somewhat contrary to the main bent of European philosophy since the Enlightenment. To put it crudely, during that epoch theorists often tended to treat all non-human terrestrial matters as purely business for Science, while dismissing the idea of spiritual transactions with anything non-human to a less respected box called Religion – a box that could itself be consigned to the care of History, Anthropology, Sociology and perhaps Psycho-Analysis.

Thus many tidy-minded philosophers were able to avoid dealing at all with the awkward problems about 'man's place in Nature' which had worried their predecessors. Less tidy-minded and more thoughtful ones, however, found that the segregation was not working. The problems tended to come back in different forms, often harder ones. For one thing, neither Science nor Religion remained safely cordoned off from other philosophical issues. Science in particular expanded in a way that made it impossible to isolate it.

It raised huge questions about topics such as cosmology, time, evolution and the ultimate constitution of matter – questions which could not possibly be confined to their private box in the 'philosophy of science' since they impinged also on the meaning of life. Relations began to emerge between some central scientific concepts and some of those formerly supposed internal to religion – notions such as order and our faith in it, the source of order, finitude, destiny, direction. As these connexions emerged, these vast topics naturally and inevitably attracted – in the minds of scientists as well as other people – the kind of awe that had traditionally been associated with religion.

POLARIZATION PROBLEMS

All this posed a difficulty for the simple and satisfying idea that these two provinces of thought were quite simply rivals. For more than a century now, our culture has largely swallowed the positivistic pattern which treats religion and science as competitors, as distinct, alternative attitudes belonging to separate tribes – one tribe being childish and the other mature. Still worse, if one asks what the two tribes stand for, the answer often concentrates entirely, not on religion as such, which is a fairly universal human phenomenon, but on a single doctrine of fundamentalist Christianity.

It centres on a particular factual account of the origin of the physical universe. When did that event take place? Was there a fabulous being designing it, a being who will now look after us, or was there not? Other issues, such as present attitudes to the meaning of life and the nature of the soul, are not seen as being relevant because they're not scientific business. So a lot of people – not only professional scientists – see these two very different human concerns (science and religion) as essentially just two rival historical views about the origin of the physical world – a false one and a true one. The last thing they expect is to see new, disorganized forms of religion springing up under the auspices of science.

For people with this approach, 'science' seems simply to mean the honest acceptance of facts, opposing a kind of 'religion' which licenses childish wish-fulfilment. Even writers who are pointing out the limitations of science often seem resigned to this view of the matter. Thus Brian Appleyard, in an otherwise quite sensible recent book about the dangers of scientism, complained that '*the heartless truths* of science destroy the soul of mankind'. That sentence was even put forward as the motion to be discussed, and was defended by the author, at a widely-advertised debate in London to publicize his book.[1]

But truths do not destroy souls. Truths can, of course, be heartlessly told, but they can't, themselves, be heartless. The trouble about science is absolutely not that it tells unwelcome truths, but that its prestige obscures other truths which are every bit as well established and important – for instance, the truth that, quite literally, people can't live by bread alone and that without vision they perish, so that our imaginations will continue to work, and to influence our thinking powerfully, whether we pay any attention to them or not.

To repeat: the trouble with science-worship is its exclusiveness. Obsession with scientific method makes people ignore other topics and forget that there are any other mental disciplines. It distorts the whole mental scene. It can even lead to the telling of dangerous *un*truths under the name of science, as we shall shortly see.

The main 'challenge of science' today for people concerned about humane and spiritual values is surely the need to explode this bizarre notion that science – meaning the physical and social sciences, which together make up quite a small section of our knowledge – has a monopoly of truth, while religions and other provinces of thought need not even aim to be truthful.

This notion rightly makes many scientists themselves very uncomfortable. In May 1993, the British magazine *New Scientist* ran an interesting controversy on the relations between science and religion. Scientists who took religion seriously and knew something about it attacked this crude polarization very effectively. But the defenders of the stereotype evidently couldn't really hear their arguments at all. Throughout the dispute, these people saw the issue as a simple tribal battle against the Church, a straightforward call for heroic honesty, just as early Enlightenment warriors such as Hobbes and Hume did. They weren't looking at the imaginative dramas that actually surround the idea of 'Science' at the present day at all. But I think we need to look at them.

REVERSING THE ROLES?

It is really hard to shift these entrenched stereotypes. In the early 1980s it occurred to me to try a different approach to that problem, when I was asked to give a talk at a conference on 'Evolution and Religion'. At that time, I had been getting interested in certain curiously intense purple passages about evolution that I noticed in serious scientific books – passages which seemed to me to smell of incense and hymn-books rather than of the laboratory. Just to give their flavour briefly here, I quote one which appears unexpectedly at the end of a perfectly reputable book by a molecular biologist about the chemical origins of life on earth.

Having carefully discussed the detailed workings of the primal soup, the author suddenly asks, 'What of the future?' He explains that evolution is essentially an increase in intelligence and then he confidently predicts what is to come:

He [man] will splinter into types of humans with differing mental faculties that will lead to diversification and separate species. From among these types, a new species, Omega man, will emerge, either alone, in union with others, or with mechanical amplification to transcend to new dimensions of time and space beyond our comprehension – as much beyond our imagination as our world was to the emerging eucaryotes ... If evolution is to proceed through the line of man to a next higher form, there must exist within man's nature the making of Omega man ...

Omega man's comprehension and participation in the dimensions of the supernatural is what man yearns for himself, but cannot have ... What comprehension and powers over nature Omega man will command can only be suggested by man's image of the supernatural.[2]

I accordingly spoke about these prophecies at the conference, and later discussed them in a little book, under the title of *Evolution as a Religion*. I want to make it clear that this move was not just a debating tactic, a way of saying 'you're another'. It was designed to point out how unrealistic it is to try and isolate science from the rest of thought and the rest of life. It was meant to show how all our thought – including science – arises out of imagination, how deeply we need to acknowledge that debt and to grasp its consequences.

Of course the book-title wasn't quite right. These passages don't actually deliver the kind of coherent, more or less integrated system that makes up a complete religion. Instead, they express a loose, undisciplined assortment of the motives and images that normally go to form religions. Normally, when materials of this kind grow together into a religion, they get disciplined so as to fit into a more or less integrated way of life. But here, colourful impulses and images seemed to be erupting unofficially, without any such controlling context.

In fact, what made me notice them in the first place was that they actually conflicted with their context. They said things which were flatly contrary to current biological theory. The kind of 'evolution' that these passages celebrated was not Darwin's, but Lamarck's. It was a predestined, all-embracing upward surge of progress culminating in Homo Sapiens and destined to carry him on up to indefinite vistas of future glory. That concept is quite foreign to modern science. Yet it was being expounded in scientific language, with no indication that the writers knew they were moving to a different topic, and with great excitement, as something of tremendous importance.

WHY IT MATTERS: THE NEED FOR VISIONS

This odd phenomenon is not just a chance aberration. It is a sign of a much wider confusion. 'Science' has been exalted as the one central path of thought, the core of human wisdom, the sole form of guidance needed for 'a scientific age'. In effect, it has been looked to as a source of ethics. Yet it has certainly not been expanded in a way that could allow it to give this sort of guidance. Indeed, all through the last half-century the idea of science has been steadily narrowed. Ideological prophets such as Marx and Freud, who did claim to give guidance, are now no longer considered 'scientific'. Officially, science is now supposed to deal only in facts, to be an objective, non-ideological and value-free memory-store, a sternly economical pattern of information, due to replace the fanciful wish-fulfilments offered by Religion. That claim to objectivity is the source of its tremendous authority.

But of course science has always been much more than that. Scientists don't just collect facts. They relate them and place them within a wide imaginative picture, which forms part of a still wider picture of life as a whole. To do this, Science always has and needs its own, very forceful, imaginative vision. If it isn't furnished with a sensible vision, it cannot fail to gather a wild one instead. And that is what has lately been happening.

In the seventeenth century, in the first epoch of modern science, a vision of this kind did indeed form part of it. It was a vision descended from that of Plato's *Timaeus*, a vision of a vast clockwork, devised and run by an already familiar God, but a very intellectual one, a god who now was a far better and busier geometer than the creator whom Plato had envisaged. This very powerful and impressive scheme did allow some accommodation between the scientific and religious aspects of life. But as time went on, many hitches and difficulties developed within it, most obviously about human free-will. These were usually resolved by dropping the designer. As Laplace said when Napoleon asked him about God, 'I do not need that hypothesis'.

In the nineteenth century, therefore, a darker and much more mysterious picture developed. This picture shows the machine working alone in a vacuum without a source. Mechanism itself became the ultimate reality. Providence was withdrawn and people who found this hard to accept were dismissed as moral weaklings. More lately, however, that mechanistic picture too has lost its standing for a quite different reason. The clockwork pattern no longer works for modern physics. Physicists don't now see mechanism as the final cosmic truth, only as one more metaphor with a limited use.

That change ought surely to show us how odd the nineteenth-century model always was. The idea of a *machine* is essentially the idea of something planned and intended. The notion of an unplanned, independent spontaneous machine doesn't really make much sense. So people have always tended to dramatize it by adding some kind of fate-figure behind it, a shadowy purposive designer in the background – either a benign one, such as Evolution, or a sinister one such as Ruthless Necessity or the Selfish Gene. In this way the machine model has always tended to degenerate into superstitious fatalism.

Such as it was, however, that model did provide some sort of a general background. Without it, theorists no longer have any coherent imaginative picture that can bring all human concerns together. Yet the hunger for that unifying pattern doesn't go away. In fact, the confusions of our age probably make that hunger still stronger. And the huge successes of technology still lead us to expect science to provide this pattern.

That is why scientists are now looked to as priests and prophets. That is why a highly technical scientific book like Stephen Hawking's *Brief History of Time* can become a runaway best-seller, simply because it contains a few casual claims to cast light on 'the mind of God'. (It is hard, isn't it? to imagine a book by a theologian who had actually thought about that subject having this kind of success today . . .) And that, finally, is why some scientists, even quite eminent ones, have been meeting this demand by producing superstitious, fantasy-ridden variations on the machine-myth that are meant to supply a new meaning for life.

A SHARED PROBLEM

Now of course, in discussing all this, it is essential that we non-scientists don't conduct a war against science. This is *not* a tribal issue. It's a problem for everybody. Today's scientists are not to blame for the tremendous wave of prestige which now leads people to expect spiritual guidance from them, along with lasers and Prozac and a cure for cancer. It is not their fault, either, that their work is now so specialized that they get neither the time nor the training to reflect much on how their work fits into the rest of life.

In the past, some scientists and also some philosophers, from Bacon to H.G. Wells, did indeed build and encourage these romantic hopes. They created 'scientism', the undiscriminating faith in science as the cure for all ills and the right way to answer all questions – a faith which has had huge influence in our time. For instance, Pandit Nehru, addressing the National Institute of Science of India in 1960, said:

It is science alone that can solve the problems of hunger and
poverty, of insanitation and illiteracy, of superstition and dead-
ening custom and tradition, of vast resources running to waste,
of a rich country inhabited by starving people.[3]

Science alone? No decent laws needed, no honest politicians and
administrators, no common-sense, no congenial way of life . . .?
People accepted these extraordinary claims because they were dazzled
by the vision of omniscience, by the idea that, as the philosopher
Rudolf Carnap put it: 'There is no question whose answer is in principle unattainable by science.'

This wild claim still has its vocal champions, who do surely now
bear a serious responsibility for prolonging its reign. But the trouble
now isn't just that these champions exist. It is that all the rest of us,
whether inside or outside science, are influenced to some extent by
this hope – or fear – that science somehow does have the fundamental answer to everything.

In the two books that I wrote about this, I thought it worthwhile
to expose this strange over-confidence simply by pointing out how
contrary some of its excesses are to the official findings of science
itself. As I say, these ideas are not just personal quirks. They are the
tip of a much larger iceberg, an imaginative picture of science which,
like all such imaginative pictures, has an influence far beyond the
official doctrines that are supposed to underlie it.

Though only a few eminent writers spell out these fantasies fully, it
is clear that many more entertain them half-consciously and see in
them some hope of escape from the present daunting situation of our
planet. (Thus, NASA is currently funding research on how to spend
100,200 years terraforming Mars, to which some people would like
to move.) But *our present situation is surely already too dangerous to
allow this kind of distraction*. If the ground floor is already flooded,
we had better attend to the pumps rather than flattering ourselves
with hopes of a celestial future.

False hopes tend to spring up and flourish where there is no coherent
background community to criticize them. And unfortunately, modern
scientific education is so specialized (especially in English-speaking
countries) that it simply doesn't provide that critical community. It
doesn't train its students to weed and garden their concepts. Many
individual scientists dislike these fantasies. But they don't think it is
their business to answer them, because they regard that as a hobby
for amateurs. They may express disgust over coffee, but they're not
going to write to the journals, as academics in other disciplines surely

would do over absurdities of this calibre. (Would a historian ever get away with this kind of nonsense?)

IMAGINATION MATTERS

The point is that imaginative vision isn't a luxury, an extra, an irrelevance, a childish taste that adult scientific heroes can dispense with. It is a central part of our mental equipment for any serious study. The narrow, positivistic approach is, of course, itself just one more imaginative picture among others, and it's a very strange one. It paints the scientist in colours which scientists found flattering as a pure intellect, a cognitive being so sternly self-disciplined as to deal only in information, needing neither imagination nor emotion, perhaps rather like Mr Spock in *Star Trek*. It leads scientists to think that both these faculties are irrelevant to their work and don't need systematic criticism.

When I started to ask questions about these excesses, I found that they were treated as a non-subject. I was told that it was bad form to take notice of what scientists wrote in their last chapters. These flights were either jokes which only a humourless person would take seriously, or they were a rather noble and sacred kind of poetry – celebrations of evolution which only a philistine would laugh at.

These two alternative explanations go rather oddly together, and neither of them seems to account for the clash between these fantasies and official scientific doctrines. But the notion of poetry did seem relevant. These passages often show great emotional force, a force that's all the more striking by contrast with the background of sober – indeed, often boring – scholarship which fills the rest of the discussion. *These are surely the passages that readers, and more especially students, are going to remember better than anything else in the book.*

Such fantasies must then surely be important to their authors as well. They have to be compensations, myths designed to supply significance, dreams that console scientists who are starved of spiritual fodder by a confused puritanism, a mistaken isolation of the intellect from the rest of life.

All this seems to be cause for some degree of alarm. In our age science is hugely important, both in practice and as a symbol. Both scientists and non-scientists need to have a clear idea of how far it extends and why it matters, what it can do and what it can't. In particular, people who suppose – as many still do – that Science can and should put Religion out of business need to notice that their picture implies direct competition between them, a place where their functions overlap.

How far does this overlap extend? How far can something called 'science' provide, not just facts, but also an ideology, a general world-view which answers questions about the meaning of life? Jacques Monod reassured scientists about this by telling them that science has indeed answered these questions because it has proved that life actually has no meaning – *except* that, for some unstated reason, it is very important to keep on doing more science.[4] In effect, this simply leaves the need to do science as constituting the whole meaning of life.

This view of Monod's is, of course, not itself a piece of science but an ideology. People accepted it, in spite of its absurdity, because they were desperately wanting one. His success just shows once more how unreal it is to try and isolate scientific thought from the rest of life. Human beings can't live without finding some sort of a meaning for their life, and they can't work seriously unless they can connect their work with that meaning. All that Monod did was to make it much harder for scientists to think about the meaning of their work, harder to relate that work in any way to the rest of life. This hopeless attempt at isolation is surely what has starved some of them to the point of including in their conception of 'Science' unregenerate and confused religious elements.

OUT INTO SPACE?

In *Science as Salvation*[5] I followed this notion of a transcendent human destiny beyond its biological expressions on our own planet out onto the cosmic scale which is held to complete it, a scale where mechanized human beings are to leave the earth in order to occupy the whole universe and perhaps to become immortal. The distinguished Marxist crystallographer J.D. Bernal, who was one of its early but still influential prophets and respectfully acknowledged as such by recent proponents, proclaimed it like this:

> Once acclimatized to space-living, it is unlikely that man will stop until he has roamed over and colonized most of the sidereal universe, or that even this will be the end. Man will not ultimately be content to be parasitic on the stars, but will invade them and organize them for his own purposes. The stars cannot be allowed to continue in their old way, but will be turned into efficient heat-engines . . . By intelligent organization, the life of the universe could probably be prolonged to many millions of millions of times what it would be without organization.

On the relation between mind and body, Bernal outdid the stark asceticism of the sternest Fathers of the Church:

> Modern mechanical and modern biochemical discoveries have rendered both the skeletal and metabolic functions of the body to a great extent useless . . . Viewed from the standpoint of the mental activity by which he [man] increasingly lives, it is a highly inefficient way of keeping his mind working. In a civilized worker, the limbs are mere parasites, demanding nine-tenths of the energy of the food, and even a kind of blackmail in the exercise they need in order to prevent disease, while the body organs wear themselves out in supplying their requirements . . . Sooner or later the useless parts of the body must be given more modern functions or dispensed with altogether.[6]

Anyone who has read C.S. Lewis's science fiction novel *Out of the Silent Planet* will recognize the scheme that was pursued there by Professor Weston.[7] Quite apart from its moral defects, this scheme is every bit as lunatic, every bit as incompatible with accepted science, as is the version of the Lamarckian theory of evolution that supplied its base. Both assume an infallible, cosmic upward escalator, quite contrary to modern biology. No dispassionate observer, whether of our own species or another, who actually tried to work out objectively what is a possible future for *Homo Sapiens* would come up with this sort of prediction at any time, let alone at the present one.

What Bernal and his followers offer isn't science. They call it science, but it is, frankly, just science-flavoured pie-in-the-sky, a huge plateful of wish-fulfilment. They promise the human race a comprehensive miracle, a private providence, a mysterious saviour, a deliverer, a heaven, a guarantee of an endless happy future for the blessed who will put their faith in Science and devoutly submit to it. (Bernal saw that some people might not submit easily, and he called for very stern measures against heretics and unbelievers.)

THE CYBERNETIC ANGLE

Since Bernal's time, however, other ways of supplying these benefits have been invented, most notably the hope that artificial intelligence will prove our saviour. Donald Michie and Rory Johnston have laid them out for us:

The world is sliding precariously close to disaster ...
Economic stagnation, poverty, rampant inflation ... wars and
rumours of wars and the threat of Armageddon permeate every
corner of the globe ... In the face of this array of problems,
we ask, *from where might answers come? Could inanimate creatures of technology possibly produce solutions to the problems it has
spawned and to myriad others that afflict humanity? Could
machines themselves conceive solutions that have eluded human
minds? The message of this book is that they can, and that in the
world of to-morrow they will* ...

This assertion is not simply dreaming by technological
optimists. It is based on fact . . . . It has long been wrongly
assumed that you can only get out of a computer what you
put in ... Now, however, it has been demonstrated incontro-
vertibly that something new can come out of computers, and
that new something is knowledge ... *We can foresee the day
when poverty, hunger, disease and political strife have been tamed
by the use of new knowledge, the product of computers acting as
our servants, not our slaves. In addition, the mental and artistic
potential of man will be expanded in ways as yet undreamt of,
and the doors of the human imagination will be opened as never
before.*[8]

Is it clear why I was reminded of hymn-books? Fans of these slim vol-
umes will, I think, see what I mean. The crude, undiscriminating
euphoria that irritates some people in hymns isn't one of the noblest
aspects of religion. But it is a common accompaniment of it all the
same.

THE SHADOWY CENTRE

We will look at this proposal in more detail in the next chapter. At
the moment my question concerns the relation that both the
anthropic promise and the cybernetic one have with some kind of
religious faith. If – so to speak – there is a religious element in the
reliance on cybernetics, what is its deity? Is it an immanent god
within us – human Intelligence itself – or can it really be just the
actual machines? That does seem distinctly madder. Does the heathen
in his blindness really bow down to wood and stone, steel and plastic and silicon? Sometimes he does seem to. And of course, any
heathen who has invested his career prospects in Artificial Intelligence

has got to insist that it is the machines, not the users, that are central for the coming revelation.

If we press the question, however, it usually turns out that what is supposed to be being venerated is still that mysterious entity, Evolution itself – evidently a descendant of Bergson's Élan Vital and Shaw's Life Force, a close relative of the Victorian idea of progress, but counting today as belonging to the sciences rather than to the arts and extended beyond the domain of Life to the whole universe. This force, we are told, is now welding machines and human minds together in an unspeakable mystic union, a state of 'hyperintelligence' which will be the Omega Point and apex of the whole cosmic process, and may itself then actually become God.[9] (Teilhard de Chardin's influence is evident here, but strangely distorted and shorn of its spiritual meaning.)

THE ROLE OF THE NUMINOUS

This odd quest cannot really be seen as a mere normal scientific speculation. It would surely not be still being pursued, and constantly described as 'exciting', if it weren't for the sense that a numinous, non-human force or entity somehow exists to be tapped here. We know by now that computers aren't actually the source of new inspiration. They have indeed proved extremely useful tools for those who know how to use them properly – that is, for people who are already original thinkers, people who already know how to ask the right questions. But for people who don't – which is most of us – they either produce essentially more of what we have got already or something worse. As the practitioners so elegantly put it, 'Garbage in, garbage out'.

What hunger, then, is the soul satisfying here? I suggested earlier that *religions develop out of a number of separate components* – distinct human motives and tendencies which can grow together and be combined in various ways. C.S. Lewis, in the first pages of *The Problem of Pain*, remarked that these various tributary components come in two main streams. On one side, there's an awareness of the numinous – of the magical, the awe-inspiring, the weird, the superhuman. On the other, there's a sense of the moral.

Many cultures, said Lewis, don't really connect these two aspects of life, and indeed it can be quite hard to connect them. But we have to do it somehow:

Non-moral religion and non-religious morality existed and still exist . . . At every stage of religious development, man may

146

rebel [against uniting them] . . . He can close his spiritual eyes against the Numinous, if he is prepared to part company with half the great poets and prophets of his race, with his own childhood, with the richness and depth of uninhibited experience. [Or] He can regard the moral law as an illusion, and so cut himself off from the common ground of humanity. He can refuse to identify the Numinous with the righteous, and remain a barbarian, worshipping sexuality, or the dead, *or the life-force, or the future*. But the cost is heavy.[10]

That is surely what is going on here. Morality of a kind has of course been invented to go with the worship of evolution as predestination, but it has always been a crude and utterly inadequate sort of morality, a morality that no one would choose for its own sake. It is merely 'evolutionary ethics' – the bizarre notion that survival of the fittest is a principle that *must* rule us because it is somehow both an unbreakable law of nature and also an all-justifying moral ideal. Thus it is our duty to make sure that the fittest survive because that is what is bound to happen in any case . . . This pathological outcrop still seems to be seen as the guiding ethic of capitalism. It is as unscientific as it is pernicious, and it's a crucial element in the moral muddle we are struggling against today.[11]

CAN WE DO BETTER?

Can we do better? Well, I think we can. A much saner, more realistic guiding vision for science itself does now seem to be developing out of our response to the environmental crisis. Many scientists are beginning to connect the awe and wonder at nature, which is actually a prime motive in their work, with their growing concern about the state of the planet. Instead of joining in the celebrations of anthropolatry, they are pointing out how hard we need to work in order to protect the rest of nature from human destruction.

We do not yet have a suitable language for expressing this kind of concern. We are still living in the Enlightenment, and Enlightenment thought has, until lately, been too deeply anthropolatrous to form one. But people are gradually beginning to forge it. Philosophers are busy trying to find a way of saying that wildernesses have value in themselves without losing touch with the accepted moral tradition. The present rather chaotic debates about 'environmental values' certainly indicate a general move in the right direction. Acknowledging awe and wonder at the natural world is surely a great deal better than flattering one's own intelligence by power-fantasies that suppose it to rule the universe.

LOVELOCK

I would like to end by mentioning one most interesting growing-point in these efforts – a case, as I think, where the imagination is being rightly used to guide and supplement scientific thinking. That case is James Lovelock's notion of Gaia. This idea gives rise to a most interesting kind of intellectual embarrassment. Gaia is a concept that plainly has both a scientific and a religious aspect. This duality puzzles a lot of people and throws some of them – especially scientists – into culture-shock. They can't stand the Gestalt-shift involved, so they simply don't look at the notion. As I said, they are used to thinking of these two concerns as irreconcilable alternatives, indeed as hostile rivals.

How have these two rival aspects come together? Well, Lovelock himself started to speak of Gaia simply because he was desperate to find a way of making people take planetary problems seriously – making them see that the biosphere as a whole could be in trouble. He says now that it was naive of him not to see that people would take this language too literally. And perhaps it was. But he has since spelt out very clearly what he does mean.

He is certainly not saying that the earth is conscious, or is capable of forming purposes. What he *is* centrally saying is that life on earth is not a loose, chance jumble of competing entities but an interdependent system, a symbiotic whole that keeps itself going by a constant interchange of benefits between its parts. That is why this whole system is something *vulnerable*. Physical matter is not, as Descartes told us, just inert valueless stuff, foreign to life. It's not a mere heap of dead, miscellaneous atoms passive to human uses. It is a mighty organized whole of which we are a part.

Recently, Lovelock has preferred to express this point through the medical model, which certainly does this particular job more neatly. This model also concentrates attention better on the scientific angle, the gritty details of the carbon cycle and the sulphur cycle and all the other specific ways in which life keeps the air and water round it in suitable shape for its own survival. Lovelock is above all a formidable atmospheric chemist. Non-scientific followers who accepted his images while ignoring these (as we say) *mechanisms* have no excuse for going on ignoring them if they actually read him.

But, through these detailed accounts, he is also making a philosophic point about the mind–body problem which I think is crucial. He is showing – against Descartes – how continuous life is with the surrounding world, how naturally and gradually it arises as part of that system, how it can't be understood without its context.[12] He is backing Aristotle against Plato, the Book of Genesis against the Manichees. (God saw that his creation was good without waiting for the seventh day to see what Man said about it. . . .) Life grows out of the soil and the atmosphere, depends on them, interacts constantly with them, shapes them and remains deeply continuous with them. It does not come crashing in as an alien invader to conquer and use them. We belong here, and belong within a whole that we need to take seriously.

Taking it seriously ought surely to resolve the Gestalt-problem that worries people over Lovelock's concept. It ought to stop us being surprised or shocked that he seems to be combining two kinds of thought – the scientific and the religious – which we have lately tried to keep separate. If we, as organisms, are really tiny parts of so vast and complex a whole, it is surely natural and right that we should regard that whole with awe and reverence, as people in many other cultures do, and that this awe should form part of the wonder with which good scientists regard Nature.

This does not, of course, mean at all that we have to see it as a personal deity. Many scientists in our own tradition, from Galileo to Faraday and Clerk Maxwell, have indeed combined this reverence for God's creation with devout Christian belief, and many still do so today. Newton himself was profoundly a theist, though he was not a Christian. Others, like Einstein and T.H. Huxley, have rejected all the religions that they found round them but have still insisted that their attitude to the universe was a religious one – which means, I think, that it was profoundly reverent. The recent attempt to suppress this kind of reverence altogether and replace it by anthropolatry does not express a demand of rationality. It is an isolated eccentricity of our own age and I think it is time that we grew out of it.

10

SUSTAINABILITY AND
MORAL PLURALISM

—— •✦• ——

VERTIGO TROUBLE

A CERTAIN sense of unreality easily infests applied ethics. Thus the bookshop lady was surprised when I asked about books on business ethics. 'Business ethics?' she said. 'Well, business books are just over there, but I think ethics must be somewhere upstairs . . .'. She could not easily relate facts and values. This problem is not uncommon. Practical affairs tend to look static, fixed and permanent. Powerful contending parties, posing various threats, seem to dominate the scene, preventing any change of direction. We see only painful, unintelligible choices of evil. At best, the question seems to be 'what's the least bad compromise available here?' By contrast, discussions of moral theory seem to look upwards, right away from the facts, at remote ideals, calling for a clarity and inflexibility which may well seem unattainable.

This sense of unreality – this impression that the two approaches can't be brought together – is particularly strong over our present environmental difficulties because the scale of the predicament is so new. The challenge is extremely surprising for the whole human race and especially so for our own recent traditions. Putting it crudely, for a couple of centuries we have been brought up to believe in progress – to expect that in principle things on earth were getting better under the guidance of our own civilization. Though we knew that we, as a culture, had moral faults, we thought that even there we were improving, and physically we certainly did not expect any very serious trouble. We were brought up to think that lapses, however bad, would be local and temporary.

Until lately, general confidence in this prospect was not seriously shaken by the various kinds of scepticism which have eroded other aspects of our thought. Belief in God might be under attack, but for most Western people belief in Man, and in the works belonging to his local avatar, stood firm. Now, however, we are called on to accept the very different story that Man himself, under his present flags, is producing actual disaster. This calls on us, not just to give up many comforts, but also to change those flags, which mark and celebrate some of our habitual ideals.

That drastic reversal, coming on top of the other sceptical trends just mentioned, calls for vigorous new thinking about values. It does not, of course, demand a completely 'new ethic' like a new hat, completely replacing the old one with something quite different, which is a meaningless idea,[1] but it does call for a great shift in perspective. We must change a habitual priority system, one which seemed relatively coherent because we were used to it, but which is no longer workable. We have to rethink the relation between our various ideals, and the way in which they are geared to life.

This effort can produce a sense of unreality leading to scepticism, dizziness and vertigo, sometimes to nausea. Bewilderment already expresses itself in various confused forms of relativism and subjectivism, which tell us to abandon all attempts at clarity[2] – prescriptions which are often summed up at present as 'Postmodernism'. This name can, however, also cover more positive rearrangements of ideals, more workable forms of pluralism, which we must look at shortly. The name 'Postmodernism' is actually a bad one, both because it is vague and because it centres on fashion. It needs always to be translated into words that are more specific and less time-bound. But the mixed batch of ideals which we have vaguely grouped together under names like 'modern' and 'advanced' is indeed central to our troubles.

FINDING THE MIDDLE GROUND

The way to deal constructively with this impression of a hopeless gap between ideals and reality is always, I think, to attend to the middle ground that connects them. We need to think about the standards that we use for compromise, and the alterations that each side must make to its demands when it understands what its opponent is driving at. At this middle level, we can see how the practical approach actually demands the idealistic one to complete it. The two levels of concern are not rivals or alternatives; they are complementary. The only hope of resolving serious conceptual clashes is to rethink them in relation to their context, noticing what can be done about the ideas involved. (There are of course simpler methods of resolution, such as combat or ordeal, which have often been tried. But they have never proved very satisfactory.)

120

Looking back, we can see how this careful rethinking has often managed to resolve dilemmas which, in their time, looked quite as incurable as our present lot. Moral thinking is not really just a luxury; it has often proved extremely effective. Thus, the religious wars of the seventeenth century did not just die out from exhaustion. They were eventually seen to be unnecessary in the light of new conceptions of toleration and the complexity of truth. Again, better notions about the nature of honour similarly removed the need for duelling.

After this kind of change has been made, however, the original difficulties tend to be forgotten, which is why we have the impression that such thought is impossible. This rethinking does undoubtedly require considerable effort. We have to sort out the various ideals that each side stands for, to see why they are clashing, and to look at their relation to our whole range of ideals so as to see a new, more workable pattern. We are forced to stand right back from our immediate problems and to get our bearings in a wider moral field. This shift is not a distraction from the real dilemmas. It is what we need if we are to take them seriously.

But of course it is always hard to do that, because the facts to be faced tend to be alarming. At present, the notion that our treatment of nature involves serious, avoidable crimes and dangers is still only very gradually seeping into public consciousness. Most of us still accept it only intermittently, and with a considerable sense of unreality. This slowness of perception is not unusual. Reading the letters and diaries of our forebears – even of very perceptive people – who lived at earlier times of rapid change, we see it constantly. We sometimes want to shout to the writers and call on them to wake up.

Thick, solid layers of habit always protect our established ways of life against criticism. And, rather surprisingly, they do not just block moral criticism. They numb the sense of danger as well. People have always farmed contentedly on the slopes of volcanoes. Christians have not been stopped from sinning by the expectation of eternal damnation. The dangers of modern weapons have not made us give up war. Habit, in fact, has extraordinary force, a force greatly exceeding the wish for self-preservation.

THE APPEAL TO EGOISM

Enlightenment thought, which we still use, has largely ignored this remarkable insensibility born of habit. It has put great trust in enlightened self-interest as the source of reform. Hobbes supposed that rational people only needed to be warned of threats against their personal safety in order to change their political ways. A similar strategy, on a larger scale, is now being used by prophets who hope to change our attitudes to nature purely by pointing out the risks that we, as human beings, are now running. The sense of 'sustainability' which just means 'protection of human use' is geared to that intention. The interest of our own species is presented as the only possible rational and parsimonious approach.

Thus, Messrs Pearce and Turner (official environmental advisers to Mrs Thatcher and her successors) raise their eyebrows to enquire:

> If inherent/intrinsic and not just instrumental value exists, what is it and how do we discover it? It seems reasonable to conclude that we either justify our acceptance of intrinsic value at an intuitive level only, or we look for support via appeals to 'expert judgment'. Both of these forms of justification seem problematic.[3]

These writers seem to find the notion that, by contrast, all values might be merely instrumental, leading to no particular end at all, quite straightforward . . . This might seem odd. But they are, of course, actually assuming that human aims, which the instruments exist to meet, are taken as given and need no discussion.

This approach gives a quite simple answer to the question why uses of wild species should be 'sustainable'. Very obviously, human beings are dependent on many of the threatened species and cannot survive without them. The word 'sustainable', now appearing in many official documents since the publication of the Brundtland Report, does signal some faint, dawning recognition of this glaring fact even among those politicians and administrators who are most thickly protected from it by the veils of official habit. It shows that former delusions about the infinity of resources, the need for an all-out war against nature and the omnipotence of the technical fix are becoming slightly weaker.

That progress towards wakefulness is, so far, immensely welcome. Enlightened self-interest is indeed a necessary component in change. Fright can certainly wake people up, and it sometimes concentrates their minds amazingly. The question is, however, how far can we rely on fright? Will it give us all the motivation we need to alter our attitudes? Does it articulate the considerations that we need to build into our changed world-picture?

This species-egoist approach has two serious limitations, which are the main subject of this chapter. One concerns the detailed policies it recommends, the other, which interests me more, concerns the human psychology that lies behind those policies. About the detailed policies, clashes are notoriously already emerging. Ingrained habits of economic thinking ensure that the idea of conserving natural resources, or 'natural capital', in quantities sufficient for human needs will be tied to a minimal level. Thus, if humans need wood, trees must be replanted, but they should always be the trees that will supply this need most quickly and economically. There is no reason to conserve existing species, and certainly none to aim at diversity as such. And after all there are a lot of kinds of trees about. So, what could possibly be wrong with universal monocultured eucalyptus?

SURGEONS, LIFEBOATS AND FIRST-CLASS PASSENGERS

This question is being constantly and shrewdly answered at present by a patient, determined squad of hard-working environmentalists. Jared Diamond does the job as well as anyone. People ask, he says:

> Could we not preserve only those particular species that we need, and let other species become extinct? Of course not, because the species that we need also depend on other species . . . Which ten tree species produce most of the world's paper pulp? For each of those ten tree species, which are the ten bird species that eat most of its insect pests, the ten insect species that pollinate most of its flowers, and the ten animal species that spread most of its seeds? Which other species do these ten birds, animals and insects depend on? . . .
>
> Consider the following analogy. Suppose someone offers you a million dollars for the privilege of painlessly cutting out two ounces of your valuable flesh. You figure that two ounces is only one-thousandth of your body-weight, so you will still have nine-hundred and ninety-nine thousandths of your body left . . . But what if the surgeon just hacks two ounces from any conveniently accessible part of your body, or does not know which parts are essential? . . . If you plan to sell off most of your body, as we now plan to sell off most of our planet's natural habitats, you are certain eventually to lose your urethra.[4]

What interests me is the difficulty that even very prudent people have in believing simple arguments of this kind. When Garrett Hardin said that privileged people today were the occupants of an overburdened lifeboat who, despite their compassion, really could not risk taking anyone else on board, he struck many readers as realistic. Somebody promptly replied that these privileged people were actually first-class passengers who had just got a warning from the people in steerage that their ship is sinking. The tendency to reply 'not at our end' does not then seem so sensible. But this image has not caught on half as readily.

The psychological quirk that blocks our imagination here has already been seen in political life with the disappointment of Hobbes's hopes. People turn out not to be anything like as prudent as Hobbes supposed. Human selfishness is indeed very powerful, but it is closely linked to human narrowness. It tends to concentrate vigorously on the present. It is not imaginative. It discounts absent scenes and remoter futures just as it discounts other people's feelings. It can be extraordinarily short-sighted. It tends to be competitive rather than co-operative, setting individual self against others, even in places where rationality urgently demands co-operation. In short, egoism is by its nature rather *un*enlightened and hard to enlighten. If it is to power real reform, it always needs a wider framework of other motives.

These other motives are, however, available. Selfishness does not actually dominate our emotional lives in quite the way that Hobbes thought. Human rationality is not a monoculture, a simple system with a single aim. It is the project of bringing together in some sort of harmony the many motives, many interests that naturally form part of human life. Moral 'pluralism' is correct in the sense that we really do have many distinct ideals. But of course we cannot just pursue them all at random. In trying to bring them together harmoniously, we need to have some sort of comprehensive world-picture, some vision of the whole within which we live and of our own relation to it.

Hardly anybody actually manages to handle human social life on Hobbes's extreme egoistic model. People are social beings who normally feel themselves to be part of a group, indeed part of many concentric and overlapping groups, with aims that are directly important to them. They often identify strongly with their various groups, and mind intensely about changing or maintaining group habits and qualities. Often they willingly sacrifice their individual interests for their groups, or for other individuals. They sometimes even die for them.

WIDER HORIZONS

But above and beyond these groups, they almost inevitably have a further sense of a wider whole, a theatre within which all groups play their part. And most cultures have not attempted to conceive that whole as exclusively a human one. This wider whole may not be something that we often think about, but the way in which we conceive it is surely crucial for our moral attitude. When this larger imaginative vision changes, the light in which we see all our various concerns is altered. Priorities shift, carrying a corresponding change in duties.

Christian morality, for instance, has certainly not been primarily a prudential, egoistic device to help individuals gain Heaven and avoid Hell. (People who have used it in that way have misunderstood it, and have usually fallen into deep trouble.) It has been meant as a way of acting that is shaped by the vision of the world as created by a loving God and lit up by love of one's neighbour. Whatever the failures of the actual institutions involved, this way of looking at things made possible many moral insights – for instance about the wrongness of slavery and infanticide – which we now take for granted, but which were not easily grasped before. The size and nature of our world-picture determines the range of our moral horizon. By altering the light in which we see our role, it always has direct, practical effects on what we feel called on to do.

THE REDUCTIVE PROJECT

Since the Renaissance, however, sages and prophets in the West have worked hard to shape our imaginative vision in a way that systematically narrows it. There has been a deliberate effort to exclude from concern everything non-human, and many supposedly non-rational aspects of human life as well. Though this campaign was aimed chiefly against the dominance of the churches, and was rooted in the horror of religious wars, it has usually taken the form of a 'humanism' that excludes non-human nature too. This is still the unquestioned creed expressed in the ministries and offices from which our society is run. Often, too, it is narrowed yet further to the economists' formula, which still defines 'rationality' in Hobbesian terms of individual self-interest.

Now it is not actually impossible to state the case for strong environmental action even in this restricted language. Though an isolated egoistic individual could probably count on free-loading for his lifetime, any wider concern, even for one's own friends and descendants, does call for marked changes. And the kind of prudence that extends to the whole human race would, if really enlightened, demand very drastic changes indeed.

This is the voice that, since the Brundtland Report, we have been hearing in the very general declarations made by governments about the importance of sustainability. But we rightly have a sense of unreality about these declarations, because we know that self-interest on this immensely public, long-term scale is not usually very enlightened. At this range, enlightened calculations tend to be too indirect to have much force, and ordinary, unenlightened sectional selfishness usually works quietly in their shadow. If prudence on this scale is to be effective, it needs to be supplemented by a much more direct, spontaneous moral feeling – in fact, by a sense of outrage.

What ended the wars of religion, and the savage treatment of heretics that went with them, was not just the wish for self-preservation, though that certainly played its part. It was also direct horror at the atrocities involved. Voltaire, though he was a prophet of reason, sounded this note of profound indignation as a persistent bass to his campaigns on this matter, and it was central to his effectiveness. It is equally so in environmental campaigning today.

WHAT DO WE REALLY THINK?

Arne Naess, who wanted to discover ordinary people's views, conducted a series of systematic interviews with them on the rights and values of animals, plants and landscapes. He reported:

> In spite of what one would guess from the way they vote (and I am speaking as a Scandinavian), there is a substantial majority with quite far-reaching ideas about the rights and value of life-forms, and a conviction that *every life-form has its place in nature* which we must respect.

In short, people are not orthodox individualists. They do not proceed atomistically outward from the demands of each separate human, demanding credentials sternly from each new suppliant who wants to be taken into the lifeboat. They do not feel like immigration officers, defending the human race against alien outsiders. Instead, they feel that they live within a vast whole – nature – which is in some sense the source of all value, and whose workings are quite generally entitled to respect. They do not see this whole as an extra item, or a set of items which they must appraise and evaluate one by one to make sure whether they need them. They see it as the original context which gives sense to their lives. It is the background they start from. From this angle, the burden of proof is not on someone who wants to preserve mahogany trees from extinction. It is on the person who proposes to destroy them.

Naess reported this work in a detailed personal letter to 110 people who were influential on national environmental policy, asking for
their comments. One in three replied, and commented very
favourably, suggesting that, at least at a personal level, they too were
much in line with Naess's 'ordinary people'. Naess concluded that
there was a considerable gap between public feeling and the principles governing official policy, a gap that should be exposed and
sharply attended to. As he put it:

> What is needed is a methodology of persistently connecting
> basic value-judgements and imperative premises with decisions
> in concrete situations of interference or non-interference in
> nature. What I therefore suggest is that those who are thought
> to be experts and scientists repeatedly and persistently deepen
> their arguments with reference to basic value-judgements and
> imperative premises. That is, they should announce their nor-
> mative philosophy of life and discuss environmental problems in
> their most comprehensive time and space frame of reference.[5]

Some recent researchers have followed up Naess's work by inter-
viewing twenty-four senior policy advisors to four European governments active in global climate change negotiations and the UNCED
process. They report:

> In response to our questions, a majority of these advisors
> articulated deeply held personal environmental values. *They told
> us that they normally keep these values separate from their envi-
> ronmental policy activities* . . . We suggest that environmental
> policy could be improved if widely held environmental values
> were articulated, validated and admitted into the process of
> policy analysis and deliberation.[6]

LOOKING OUTWARDS

The present position, in fact, is rather like what we would find in a
ministry charged with running prisons if all humane talk about what
life was like for the prisoners was banned, and proposals for reform
had always to be couched in terms of efficiency in preventing crime.
This sort of indirectness is obviously misleading and wasteful. Naess
is surely right that, on environmental questions, we need to stop
being embarrassed about admitting that we are not all petty-minded
egoists. As the recent researchers put it, we need this clearer moral

position if we are to avoid situations in which 'decisions based on short-term goals and narrow interests lead to longer-term outcomes desired by no one'.[7]

Of course prudential arguments are important and must be stated. But the attempt to reduce the whole of morality to them is simply silly. We are creatures whose very nature constantly points us outwards towards questions and ideals that lead far beyond our own lives. The crucialness of this outward leading is commonly taken for granted in discussing the value of science, of art and of exploration, particularly the exploration of space, and of an enterprising approach generally. It is also assumed to be natural in the extension of compassion to the borders of the human species.

People who ask, as Pearce and Turner do, how there can possibly be inherent or intrinsic value need to have their noses rubbed in such cases. When a doubt actually does arise about the value of a particular province such as science or art, we are not – as they suggest – left gaping helplessly. We look at the various aims of this activity in some detail, and see how they relate to those of other important human activities. Though there is never complete agreement on such matters, much sensible thinking is readily available. There are adequate maps for finding our way around the topic. We note the place of this particular activity in human life and in a wider firmament of values. Of course the enquiry is a vast and complex one, but it is not a blank. In thinking about it, we shall not fall dumb in the way that they suggest unless we have decided in advance that all thought about values is vacuous – a view which the Logical Positivists did indeed suggest in a euphoric moment, but which doesn't really make much sense in a world where the relative value of different things continually needs to be discussed.

Asking about the value of the whole within which all other valuable things have their place does indeed raise rather different problems. But they are not problems which can be solved by ruling that this whole is valueless. What does seem to happen here is that the word 'value' is reaching its limits. This word is in any case somewhat polluted by its constant use in economic contexts and other cost-benefit calculations, where it reverts to its literal meaning of 'price'. G.E. Moore, solemnly discussing the comparative 'values' of various large-scale states of affairs, managed to give an uncomfortably condescending impression of a distinguished connoisseur pricing pictures in an exhibition.[8] He wrote as if he stood in a secure, neutral, outside position, evaluating these things as an expert. But that is not a human situation at all.

MORE WORDS ARE NEEDED

The trouble surely is that, as we speak of things further and further out from ourselves, it gets steadily more suitable to speak in terms of awe, reverence, respect, wonder or acceptance, and steadily less satisfactory to use a word like 'value' whose original use is in describing everyday objects we might buy and possess. (A 'valuer' is, in ordinary life, just a man whom the insurance company sends round to check on your claim.) I do not mean that this word cannot be used. In outspoken metaphors, like Jesus' story of the merchantman seeking the 'pearl of great price', it can work well. No doubt today the word *value*, like *rights*, can be used without danger at the everyday level. It may well be quite an appropriate word for the kind of public statements that are often now needed. But the philosophers who are now getting each other into muddles about the intrinsic or inherent value of non-human items are trying to make this single word bear far more weight than it can stand.

Their real problem is not, as they think, just one of fitting a few familiar terms together to produce a smooth, simple surface within moral philosophy. It is the big metaphysical and moral problem of what attitude creatures like ourselves ought to take towards the cosmos within which we are so small a part. It is an open-ended problem, where the most we can usually do is to get rid of certain pernicious elements that have crept in and infested our attitudes. The word 'value' has been used, by moral theorists as well as economists, to do a reductive job here, to simplify our status by exalting it. Thus used, it suggests that we have only to think about the satisfaction of certain selected human 'needs', which we shall, of course, define in terms that suit our current culture. That is why theorists like Pearce and Turner are so mystified by talk of 'values' which are not clearly reducible to such needs.

Moore and many other moral theorists have used the word 'value' as a central weapon in the campaign to assert the self-sufficiency of Man – to defend him against seeming to have any need of religion. They have observed that serious attitudes to the whole cosmos do tend to be religious, and because institutionalized religions have often been harmful, they have wanted to resist that trend. But in doing so, they have set up a form of anthropolatry that is every bit as superstitious, as arbitrary and as over-confident as any of the religions they wanted to avoid. This unreal exaltation of Man has played a key part in bringing us to our present environmental crisis. We need to do all we can to clear it out of the conceptual schemes we must use in our attempts at salvage.

CONFUSED REDUCTIVISM

This kind of English-speaking moral philosophy, characteristic of the later Enlightenment, has had another, more general fault which is still giving us trouble. It is the tendency to insist on conceptual monoculture – on bringing all moral questions together under simple headings, reducible ultimately to a few key terms. It is felt to be scientific, but it isn't. Utilitarianism began this over-tidy enterprise, and, a few decades back, linguistic philosophers managed to narrow down the 'moral words' for a time to two – 'right' and 'good'. No doubt clarity is always a gain, but you can't till fields with a nail-file. Philosophers fairly soon noticed that this kind of thing was unhelpful. They now use a much larger and more flexible toolkit.

But they do still tend to get obsessed by particular words. They have, for instance, repeatedly piled far more problems onto the concepts of 'rights' and 'justice' as well as 'value' than those words can stand, instead of looking round to see what other notions might be helpful. (What about 'importance'?) And they also have a tendency, dating from their most rule-bound epoch, to treat things as alternatives which are demonstrably not alternative but complementary – to dispute about whether we should use knives or forks instead of asking how we should combine them.

This divisiveness has already made trouble on environmental issues. Fierce debate broke out for a time between philosophers campaigning on behalf of animals and others supporting wildernesses – as if these concerns were simply rivals, rather than interdependent elements in a larger problem, elements which must be intelligently brought together. And there is now an equally irrelevant competition going on between various simple answers to the general question why we should bother about any of these things. The tendency is to say, 'We know that we ought to be concerned about the environment, but *we don't know why* until we find some single, simple explanation', and then to pursue the matter by backing some sweeping 'moral theory' intended to validate all duties wholesale.

YES, BUT *WHICH* GENERAL PRINCIPLE?

This narrow disputatiousness is obviously likely to obstruct attempts to answer questions about the general principles to which we should appeal. The notion that there is just one right set of principles is a mere distraction. We need to remember how big the questions are. We are bound to need many partial answers to them; no single password can possibly clear up the matter. This is particularly obvious when we have to turn hastily to these issues after having neglected them. But even in the long run, the place they should occupy in human life is never going to be simple. It must demand more, not less, conceptual schemes to describe it than we now use.

This would, after all, be true even on moral topics with which we are much more familiar. If somebody asks, 'But why should we bother about our children?' or, 'Why have art?' or, 'Why, really, shouldn't I kill you?', many people will be somewhat stuck for an answer. This is not (as cocky graduate students tend to think) because these people don't know the answer, but because they know too many answers.

Such general queries make no sense unless we know just why they are being asked. Where does the particular questioner stand? What is being presupposed? What unusual conditions are raising the question and making it real? What good reasons for *not* bothering are being brought forward? What other background concerns are still being taken for granted? What specific conflicts, in fact, are we dealing with? Without this background, such questions are vacuous. General 'moral theories' – such as Utilitarianism or Rawls's Theory of Justice – become vacuous too when they are wheeled up to answer them.

These theories have their place in explanation, but it is (again) a more limited one, in helping to arbitrate particular conflicts between other possible principles, not in ruling over all of them. No theory has the absolute dominion which Utilitarianism so mistakenly claimed. None can make the whole moral scene intelligible. And of course when we turn to questions about the environment, these theories have still less prospect of being helpful, because all of them – including even Rawls's – were devised before the issue really came onto people's moral horizon. Enlightenment thinking has never said much about it. And the scale on which it confronts us now – the genuine planetary danger – is something unparalleled in the history of our species. There is no use in scouring our recent predecessors for ready-made solutions to it.

HOW THEN SHOULD WE TALK?

This does not mean, of course, that earlier ideas cannot be helpful. Since ethics grow naturally, rather than being bought like hats, there is already much material which we can gather, use and foster, rather than inventing some astonishing novelty. When we ask whether principles such as respect for life, stewardship and species' rights can be used, the answer is surely, Yes – and plenty more. All have their own advantages and drawbacks. All will need further development, and all will surely get it as we think harder about these matters. All overlap on an enormous area of the action that is necessary. All, however, suit some contexts better than others.

For instance, the language of rights has a particular resonance for Americans, who may well accept it without question. In Europe, and perhaps elsewhere, its shortcomings in certain kinds of context are more obvious. Some brief explanation may therefore be needed to show how using it outside its familiar political and legal context is, in fact, unobjectionable. Again, talk of 'stewardship' readily suggests a God in the background; can atheists accept it? They surely can if it is pointed out that we are stewards for our posterity. And so forth.

Similarly over differences of culture, these clashes, on the whole, seem to affect relatively minor matters. Simply because things are so bad, the main campaign ought not really to be divisive. Differences between the Western outlook and others should surely not be too troublesome this time, because we see that it is we ourselves who have, so far, been most out of step. Cultural imperialism at this point would be ludicrous. The distinctively Western anthropolatry of recent tradition is exactly what we need to abandon. We have indeed diffused this attitude widely, which makes trouble for us now. But many other cultures have not altogether lost the more viable views which they had before they listened to us. Among the larger, more dominant cultures, this was clearly true of Japan and India, and to some extent also of Islam. China may be more of a problem, but then it is so on other moral issues too, such as human rights. For such cases the prudential, anthropocentric notion of 'sustainability' is always there to fall back on. Anyway, we must all be prepared to learn from one another, rather than shutting ourselves into supposedly separate cultural boxes.

If we ask, 'does any of the proposed principles have a claim to be universal?' my answer would be, 'certainly not in the sense of winning a competition, set up by moral philosophers, for a perfect, final, all-purpose formula'. But then that quest was always a mistaken and trivial one. The kind of universality that can reasonably be sought seems to be a wide appeal to thoughtful people, coherent with the other ideals that they accept – an appeal strong enough to lead to action, and rational enough to fit in with important elements in existing morality. On all major moral questions such appeals have many elements. They are made in different terms according to the kind of issue involved and the particular public addressed. Of course the relation between these different conceptual schemes must be watched and thought out carefully. But moral pluralism of this kind is neither confused nor dishonest. It is simply a recognition of the complexity of life. The idea that reductive simplicity here is particularly rational or 'scientific' is mere confusion.

12

ARTIFICIAL INTELLIGENCE
AND CREATIVITY
—— ·◆· ——

WHAT KIND OF RESCUE?

IN THE last chapter, we glanced at the project of bringing in Artificial
Intelligence (AI) to rescue the human race from its present perils
and possibly to carry it on a predestined journey towards ultimate
perfection. And we began to ask: What kind of hope is this? Is the
project essentially just a practical device, like an attempt to find a better insecticide or contraceptive? In that case, the machines would still
be the instruments of human aims, the means to answering our own
questions. Or is it something more visionary than this? Is it meant to
bring some extraneous, extrahuman mind to help us, some kind of
intelligence that perceives, not just means, but also ends, ideals to
which we are blind? Is it going to bring us wisdom about values?

People who prophesy salvation by alien beings from distant planets
usually seem to have in mind this second kind of help. What they
hope for is something more potent than practical advice, but it is
also something that demands a much higher price. In order to co-
operate with these strange helpers, we would have to do more than
just passively accept their wisdom. We would have to learn to share
it. We should be called on to do things that had never occurred to
us, perhaps things that we ourselves did not want.

These beings would be offering a deep transformation of our inner
attitudes as well as of our institutions, a transformation of our personal lives such as might be made by a new moral, political or religious system. The position would differ from a mere offer of practical
help, in rather the same way in which – on the individual scale – the
offer of psychotherapy to an unhappy person differs from an offer of
money. Psychotherapists do indeed assure us that they are going to
bring us to what we really want. But if we are to accept this we have
to have faith in them as somehow qualified to do so.

151

If the machines are expected to fill that sort of role, they will be figuring as new characters in the human drama, as indeed aliens in science fiction usually do. Most of what goes wrong at present is due to bad human choices. So it seems that these new characters must be able to alter those choices. They will have to be quasi-people or super-people with creative powers capable of deeply changing the social scene. They will need to be able to propose aims which are not yet ours and to ask questions of a kind that we would not have thought of asking. They must intervene. They must play the kind of spiritual role that great human reformers do and play it on a scale which at present seems far beyond the scope of any human reformer. And if they do indeed have these powers, we shall want to be sure that they will always use them for good ends – ends that we can see as good – and not, as powerful humans so often do, for bad ones.

Writers who promise salvation by AI often do not seem to notice the huge gap between these two different kinds of help. (In this casualness, they simply reflect the deep, chronic over-concentration on means and the neglect of ends which is characteristic of our age.) They advertise the practical usefulness of the proposed machines and their creative potential indiscriminately, as if both contributions would be equally welcome. It is worthwhile looking again at Donald Michie and Rory Johnston's offer. After summarizing current threats, the authors ask:

> In the face of this array of problems . . . from where might answers come? Could inanimate creatures of technology possibly produce solutions to the problems it has spawned, and myriad others that afflict humanity? Could machines themselves conceive solutions that have eluded human minds? The message of this book is that they can, and that in the world of to-morrow they will.
>
> This assertion is not simply dreaming by technological optimists. It is based on fact . . . It has long been wrongly assumed that you can only get out of a computer what you put in . . . Now, however, it has been demonstrated that something new can come out of computers, and that new something is knowledge . . .
>
> We can foresee the day when poverty, hunger, disease and political strife have been tamed through the use of new knowledge, *the product of computers acting as our servants, not our slaves.* In addition, the mental and artistic potential of man will be expanded in ways as yet undreamt of, and the doors of the human imagination will be opened as never before.[1]

152

WHY SMARTNESS IS NOT ENOUGH

Discussion of claims like these often gets bogged down in debates about possibility – about the chances that certain particular developments can actually be made. Since these hoped-for landmarks are so distant, nothing definite can be said about them. So the cry is often that, since we have only just started on this journey we must have more faith. We shall never get far if we are too cheese-paring and cautious.

The question is, however: why faith in *this*? Why should we start in this direction at all? Why are these machines the best candidates, or even possible candidates, for the job of rescuing us? It is not impressive to say that they will give us new knowledge. Knowledge is not something we are short of. The current information explosion notoriously gives us far more of that than we can handle already. Unless the right questions are asked and the right answers somehow picked out of the welter, more new information is not going to help us. Why should computers be particularly good at this selection?

The usual answer is that the machines will be more intelligent, smarter, cleverer, so they can select the right facts. But intelligence in the simple sense of problem-solving capacity is not something that we are at all short of either. There are plenty of clever people about; the trouble is that they don't necessarily do what is needed. Very high intelligence is running to waste all around us in neurosis, alcoholism and depression, in feuds and organized crime, in various kinds of obsession and now through special sinks provided for it called computer games.

What we need is not more problem-solving capacity but the ability to pick out the right problems to solve. The need is not for more brains but for a better use of brains, a better use which would have to flow from a more sensible attitude to life.[2] Since computers will still be programmed by people, it is not obvious why silicon should be likely to improve on flesh and blood in this matter.

HOPES OF HARMONY

A more interesting reason for the project may emerge from Michie and Johnston's remark that this new knowledge will be 'the product of computers acting as our servants, not our slaves'. This sounds like the hope, not of novelty or cleverness but of a new sort of co-operation. Computers don't answer back. They don't strike, they don't argue, they don't quarrel among themselves; they do what they are told. So they will be content to sort out the means, leaving *us* to choose the ends. This makes it seem possible that new schemes could be worked out without the constant friction, the gaps and misunderstandings and doubts and dislikes and disagreements that do indeed so deeply hinder every human enterprise. And yet (say the authors) they will not be slaves.

This surely has to mean that they will be able to criticize, able to disagree, able to misunderstand. But if they can criticize, they will have to be taken seriously as responsible independent contributors. They must then be treated with respect as colleagues. And this would bring back all the problems of human relations. What happens when they disagree with us? And who, in any case, are *we*? Have disagreements among the humans in charge been eliminated?

There is surely no halfway house here. It is not possible to treat something as both a tool and a colleague. These authors' use of the terms *servants* and *slaves*, terms which sound so odd today, shows the falsity of the attempt to bridge this gap. Employers are indeed always hoping that they can use a human being simply as a tool, and profit by the full use of his or her faculties, without the bother of treating him or her with respect. But this trick never works.

So long as either machines or people are subordinates that can simply be overruled, they are still tools. Machines in this situation are not supposed to be conscious and they raise no social problem. But it is then useless to expect from them the kind of salvation that involves thought about ends, about priorities, about values as well as means. Most notably, this means that they cannot help us to resolve conflicts about the priority between different values. And such conflicts, either between groups or between individuals or within each person, are a prime source of our troubles.

These limits on their use have surely already become clear. Of course it is true that computers, used as tools, have been of tremendous help in every branch of enquiry, often making possible entirely unexpected developments. But these same tools have also played a crucial part in the development of weaponry, of organized crime, of modern methods of torture and of the electronic money-market that at present compounds all our social problems. The power that they give us is a flexible one, a resource that can be used equally for any kind of purpose. They are reversible, directionless, morally neutral in just the same way as the knowledge and the cleverness that we have already mentioned are. This means that, unless the human race in general grows wiser, they are bound to contribute to our problems at least as fast as they do to our solutions and – since it is usually easier to do harm than good – often much faster.

154

George Bugliarello has an interesting and rather different scheme for electronic salvation in which the hope of co-operation is still more central. His idea is that computers will not just agree with their users but will bring all those users into agreement with each other as well, thus diffusing harmony through their networks over the whole globe and eventually forming a whole in which the relation between individual users is much like that between neurons in a single brain:

> [At this point] the global networks I have described . . . begin to constitute a global brain . . . We can thus begin to talk of a hyperbrain . . . and we can begin to talk of hyperintelligence as the synthesis of biological and social intelligence made possible by their interaction with machines . . . It is not only the vastness of the interconnections, but also their design, speed and simultaneity, and the power and architecture of each node that, taken together, offer the possibility of a quantum step in bio-social intelligence that warrants the term hyperintelligence . . . The hyperbrain and hyperintelligence may be viewed as a new step in the evolutionary development of our species.[3]

This stage would, he prophesied, be reached during the decade before the end of the twentieth century, everybody on earth having by then been supplied with a computer.

Bugliarello expected this to work because he noticed that a surprising degree of harmony was often found among the users of existing computer networks. This cheerful phenomenon may, however, have been due to three facts:

1 people did not join such networks unless they already had a purpose in common,
2 the network usually dealt only with that shared purpose, and
3 anyone who did become dissatisfied could leave a computer network far more easily than they could have left any more bodily kind of association.

These conditions evidently did reign among the rather small networks where this way of life started – a regime which is already becoming a subject for nostalgia among many practitioners as friction mounts on the larger scale of the Internet. But as soon as conflicting aims, personalities, interests and habits of mind are introduced – as soon as any real negotiation has to be done – things become very different. Agreement is then no easier to secure in electronic life than it is in streets, offices, villages and sitting-rooms. Bugliarello does say that we will have to be careful about 'pathologies . . . lack of integration of the different states of the brain' (p. 33). But he gives no hint at all about how he thinks we can cure them.

This remarkable casualness about the central problems of human relations has become normal in electronic Utopias. Typical examples can be studied in Marshall T. Savage's book *The Millennial Project: Colonizing the Galaxy in Eight Easy Steps*.[4] Its author presupposes that complete social harmony will be available for his cosmic project, combined with equally perfect freedom:

> Humans are like specialized cells in a macro-organic superorganism . . . We are cosmic brain-cells . . . In brain tissue . . . each individual brain-cell is free to respond to stimuli in its own way . . . This interactivity is the key to our intelligence and it will be the key to true democracy . . . Pre-conditioned by our past experience of the world, our prejudices throw up objections like flak over Baghdad. 'No-one will be in charge'. 'Who will make the decisions?' . . . 'It will be utter chaos!' Exactly. And that is the point. Pure democracy allows the body politic to tap into the ultimate driving engine of Cosmos – Chaos.
>
> (pp. 364–6)

Savage explains that this spontaneous unanimity can be expected to produce unvaryingly benign results on the model of the Chicago Stock Exchange.

If we don't share this confidence, what hopes can we have? In the course of human history, quite a number of useful suggestions have been made both about how to resolve particular disagreements and how to control disagreements in general. Such suggestions are often called creative. But – to mention something obvious – so far, these useful suggestions have all been made by *people*, not by machines, and have been based on those people's experience of human life. They have often called for new ways of looking at that life. Their proposers needed to forge, practise and try out these ideas in their own lives before they could recommend them to other people. A good example is the new concept of tolerance which was hammered out in the later Enlightenment as a way of arbitrating differences of religion. But that, too, grew out of hard experience within human life. The question that now arises is, is it possible for machines as well as human beings to put forward creative suggestions of this kind?

PROBLEMS ABOUT CREATIVITY

Creativity is not a wholly clear concept.[5] At this point we should perhaps ask three questions about it:

1 What, if anything, is creativity?
2 Does its occurrence in our universe pose a special problem for science?
3 If so, can Artificial Intelligence help to solve that problem?

In discussions of Artificial Intelligence the word creativity has often been used to mark out a disputed territory with a view either to conquering it for the machines or to vindicating its independence from them. This approach tends to involve a rather naive view of minds and how to explain them. It inclines to see creativity as a small, anomalous residue of human thought, distinct from the rest of it, the awkward bit that is left over when all the rest has been explained by science. The word 'science' too has here a special, old-fashioned sense, related to the traditional idea of a machine.

This tradition belongs essentially to the Age of Reason. Though the great Romantics, from Blake and Wordsworth on, protested against it, it gradually became widely accepted. Increasingly, people grew used to the idea that creativity is an isolated island of mystery in an otherwise scientifically explained world. Some of them protested that it was a large and important island. But this protest did not disturb the main reductive enterprise any more than Indian reservations could block the path of colonization. The idea that something called science – meaning essentially physics – would eventually explain the world completely gained strength throughout the nineteenth century with repeated scientific successes.

Against that tidy background, the wildness of these 'creative' areas stood out as an increasingly scandalous exception. On this reductive view, the problem of creativity was part of that already raised by free will, which was also seen as a rare, awkward, apparent exception. The question then was simply how to bring these awkward cases into line with the rest of human thought by explaining them, too, completely. And it was hoped that this could be done by producing computer programs that could duplicate their work. This would not only make the world fully intelligible, but would also solve its practical problems. The machines, fully understanding all that had been done already, could make themselves useful by actually taking over the jobs that had needed creativity, and doing them far better than people had done them.

SOMETHING WRONG?

There are two ways in which one can attack the naivety of this idea. One is to point out where it doesn't work on its own terms. The other is to say why those terms are mistaken, why it was not the right thing to try in the first place. Both points are worth making. The second, however, seems to me more important because, until it is somehow dealt with, endless time and effort will go on being wasted on trying to improve this project.

On the first path, various critics have done admirable work exploding myths, deflating hyped-up claims, carefully pointing out the difference between what can and what can't actually be done in AI laboratories. Margaret Boden, for instance, has much more chastened and realistic hopes of what can be expected from Artificial Intelligence than Michie's. She shows that even on points where the crude project may have been right in principle, it needs enormous corrections. Neither science, nor atoms, nor mechanisms, not computers are what it euphorically supposed them to be. Its claims have to be made far more subtle and far more modest.

This process can bring our reducer to the position of Donald Michie on his better days, dealing in a less numinous artificial intelligence, but still hoping that it will do much to build the New Jerusalem. Though this reducer still hopes to cram human thought into a box, he has learnt to make that box much larger, more complex and more appropriate. He can now sometimes be persuaded to spread it into a system of boxes, maybe even into a small housing estate. And, in doing this, he can sometimes be forced to recognize more realistically the size of some of the items he had hoped to compress.

However, a strong compressing, reductive enterprise is still needed for the big claims that AI will not just supply useful material, but will contribute something unique, something not otherwise available, to doing the huge things which previous human thought tried so hard to do and failed. Since (as we mentioned earlier) there is at present no shortage of humans, nor even of intelligent humans, these claims rest on the idea that AI somehow contains all the central, necessary structure of human thought completely enough to transcend it and to build structures on it which humans could not build. Only if the basic structure of human thought is small enough to be contained in that way will machine intelligence be large enough to encompass it. That is why the people who proclaim high hopes for the machines seem to themselves very positive-minded prophets, but find themselves regarded as mean-minded reducers. That is the charge that they need to meet.

THE CASE OF ART

Do matters become easier when we move from the area of general, practical salvation to the special case of art? Art is not the central field for the battles outlined in manifestos like Michie's, but it is a particularly awkward minor one, because it ought surely to be a showcase for machine productivity. The pressure of this hope has been felt from the dawn of mechanistic thinking. It surely lay behind the project of word-jumbling machines such as the ones that Gulliver observed in Laputa.

By now, confrontation with the actual achievements of AI does tend to moderate claims. Michie is actually less respectful to existing computer-produced art than Margaret Boden is,[6] though they both still tend to draw blank cheques on the future, on the ground that 'this project is still in its infancy'. This developmental excuse, however, isn't worth much. An infant grass-snake is never going to grow up to be a jackdaw nor an acorn to be a pear-tree, however long you leave them and however much research-money you provide.

On the wider question of creativity, Margaret Boden's claim is much more modest than Michie's. She states only that AI can *cast light on* human creativity, rather than being 'creative' itself. This is part of her general moderating project, which has done a great deal to make claims about AI clearer, more realistic, less abstract and Utopian. But this retreat is not really enough. We also need to follow up the second line and ask about the point of the whole reductive enterprise.

SURPRISING DETOURS

If what we are looking for is light on human thought, why is it sensible to approach this familiar topic by a detour, by looking for its reflexion in the distant and patchy mirror of mechanized calculation, rather than by looking at thought itself more directly? Why, for instance, do many people now believe that the best approach to the 'problem of consciousness' must be to devise machines which imitate conscious behaviour? Stevan Harnad, for instance, decides that the mind is 'scientifically investigable' all right, but that

> it cannot be investigated directly, the way most things are investigated. It can be investigated indirectly . . . *Scientific mind-theory is better described as reverse bio-engineering* . . . A scientific theory of mind would first have to successfully second-guess what gives creatures like us, already made by the Blind Watchmaker, *our* functional capacities.

So the road ahead of us is pretty clear for the time being, even though we have reason to believe that there is a cloud at the end of it. *For now, we need to devote our time and ingenuity to second-guessing those functional capacities until we manage to scale up to a zombie.*[7]

Zombie-making, then, is the researchers' first priority. The author, however, expects a cloud because (unlike some zombie-fanciers) he realizes that, even when the zombie-factory has done its utmost, there will be no way at all of knowing whether the product is conscious or not. He concludes resignedly:

Maybe it's safe to assume that consciousness will somehow piggyback on zombie capacity; maybe not. It might be some consolation that, if it doesn't, we shall never be the wiser. But I think it's nothing to lose sleep about, at least for a long time to come.

In that case it is surely a mystery how it can possibly be claimed that reverse-engineering is central to understanding this problem.

Would it not be extremely odd to suggest this kind of approach by simulation as a way of studying any other puzzling part or aspect of the world? The study of lightning and thunder, for instance, would not have got far if it had been pursued like this. Simulations do of course play their part in other enquiries. But they are only useful for checking details once the general nature of what is going on has been grasped. Until that has been done, imitation of externals is mere wandering in the dark.

This kind of hit-or-miss imitation is, however, a favourite method in sympathetic magic. A great deal of sorcery is reverse-engineering. Rainmakers mimic the symptoms of rain and sorcerers simulate wounds in wax images to injure their enemies. And it is often held to be important to make this mimicry realistic. But the reason why these techniques have been found to be chancy is notoriously that they rest on no real understanding of the effect to be produced. Reverse-engineering sorcerers fail because they don't know *why* the appearances they imitate appear as they do. How could an approach to conscious behaviour which mimics only its outward symptoms, carefully ignoring the direct data that we have about it, succeed any better?

THE DEMAND FOR MECHANICAL ORDER

The great attraction of this reverse-engineering approach is evidently that it can easily be seen as part of Science, in a sense where the idea of Science is closely linked to the machine-metaphor. When dedicated reducers of this kind ask for *an explanation*, they have somewhat special ideas about what can constitute one. They are not just looking for order in general. (That general search for order may well be something that is appropriate on any topic.) They are expecting a special kind of order, namely a mechanical kind – order of a sort that could in principle be invented and imposed and fully understood by human engineers. The point of putting faith in machines, and of minimizing the difference between minds and machines in order to do so, is surely to show minds as manageable by theorists in the same way that machines are manageable – namely, by taking the point of view of their inventor.

When what we want is simply control, this project is understandable. But if we want to discover what is really happening it is much less so. There seems no reason to suppose that either the world or our own minds work only by a kind of order that we are capable of understanding, still less by the kind on which we invent our machines. The evolutionary processes that produced both us and our world have not been of a kind to make that limitation in the least plausible. Our brains were (as it seems) formed largely by the practical demands made on our ancestors. Those practical demands certainly did not include the need to understand the basic order of the universe, so there is no reason to suppose we are capable of doing it. The forces producing that order were *not* human inventors. It is good luck that they have sometimes worked in ways that we can understand. But we cannot count on that luck always.

However, though there is no good reason for insisting that the world is indeed mechanical, there is an obvious motive for doing so, a motive which is not impressive. Once God is removed – and I am deliberately leaving God out of this discussion – the reason for still wanting to think of the world as constructed on mechanical principles is surely the wish to exaggerate our own powers. If there were no significant difference between people and computer programs, then those who design and alter programs could also in principle design and reshape people, and be in a position to govern their destiny. The strength of this notion today, and the cheerful vagueness with which it is treated, can be seen in a few lines from a book called *The Anthropic Cosmological Principle* by two eminent physicists.[8]

They write, in successive sentences, that 'an intelligent being . . . is fundamentally a type of computer', then that 'a human being is a *program* designed to run on particular hardware called a human body', and – still on the same half-page – that 'a living human being is a *representation* of a definite program rather than the program itself'. All they want is some formula by which to bypass any large, awkward questions about what a human being really is, and to justify treating it simply as a memory-store, transferable at will to clouds of stellar dust which will outlast the heat-death of the universe.

ON BEING ORDERLY WITHOUT BEING OMNISCIENT

Claims that we can understand our own nature completely are always mistaken, and the claim of any one particular science to monopolize this skill is a piece of megalomania. Making this claim on behalf of computer science is closely comparable to earlier mistaken attempts to do it on behalf of physics, but when it involves ignoring today's wealth of human sciences it is yet more grotesque.

Let us go back to the naive world-picture we mentioned earlier which showed this small patch of human creativity as a puzzling blot on an otherwise completely clear and intelligible universe. Both parts of this picture are wrong. Though there are many ways of making the world more or less intelligible, there is no single monolithic pattern underlying all its complexity, no single light blazing over all of it. And there doesn't have to be. The lack of a single unifying pattern does not reduce us to anarchy.

We can find different kinds of order by asking different kinds of questions. These kinds of order are related to one another in much the same way as those sets of maps that geographers put at the start of their atlases. The political, the physical and the barometric map of the same territory do not reveal a single pattern. But neither do they contradict one another, nor are they totally disconnected. We can relate them because we know that they all deal with the same piece of territory, which is something immensely more complex than any of the stories they tell about it and can accommodate all those stories without collision.

We can find links between the various kinds of order when we need them, by asking yet further kinds of questions – mainly philosophical ones, about how they are related. We get quite sufficient harmony to keep clear of the utter confusion which Enlightenment sages dreaded so much. We don't need a single tidy, unified Theory of Everything to dragoon the whole of thought, and certainly – whatever may be true in physics – for thought as a whole we are never going to get one.

THE SHADOWY SCENE

It was the naive picture, then – the landscape of sharply contrasted light and darkness – that led to unreal hopes and unreal fears. How should we conceive our nature instead? It is surely a much vaster, much more complex landscape, one which stretches away past our horizon. Parts of this landscape can't be seen at all, and a great deal of it can't be seen clearly. Other parts, however, are lit with varying success from various directions by various kinds of light. In some places several different light-sources converge, and this is often useful. But there is no single light-source, called *science*, ineluctably rising like the sun to spread its beams steadily across the whole field, and there doesn't need to be.

We did not make ourselves, and we do not know very much about ourselves. We cannot, therefore, have the kind of understanding of ourselves that we have of machines that we do make. We have only a most partial and sketchy understanding of the workings of human life, which is a far vaster and more complex affair than theorists tend to suggest. The areas of thought and life that we see as 'creative' are no more obscure than many others. They are certainly not more obscure, for instance, than our motivation or than the reasons why we often behave so badly, if those are indeed separate questions.

It is not obvious, then, why 'explaining creativity' is a project that we have to undertake. What especially needs explaining about it? Certainly we do not fully understand the source of our creative thoughts. But then, we know very little about the source of our more ordinary thoughts either. Why should we expect to?

OBJECTS AND SUBJECTS

The hopeful theorists from whom we started expect this source of thoughts to be made intelligible in the end by their science, which only hasn't done it yet because it is, of course, in its infancy. The awkward thing about this is that sciences, in the modern sense, are supposed to be 'objective', meaning that they treat what they discuss always as an object. This was the restriction which was imposed on the physical sciences in the age of Galileo. The narrow, intense focus that it gave them accounts for a great deal of their success.

But the factors that make it so hard for us to understand ourselves centre on the fact that we are *subjects*. Understanding ourselves and other people as subjects is a quite different kind of enterprise from any study of objects because the questions that it asks are different.

It needs very different methods – methods which we use every day and which take into account the subject's own point of view. We do have natural social capacities that fit us in some degree to understand ourselves and others as subjects, to grasp human motivations and the workings of the imagination well enough for practical life. But these are quite different capacities from the ones that we mostly use in studying objects, and they are ones that make the idea of a *complete* explanation look even more incoherent.

Minds, in fact, do not seem to be the kind of thing for which the idea of a complete explanation makes much sense. Perhaps it may not be too hard to accept that our understanding of our motives and imaginations is bound to be incomplete. But we need to add, what may be more alarming, that it won't be made more complete by anything that can be called, in the contemporary narrow sense, 'science' – that is, by any method that is wholly objective. The social sciences, when they deal with this area, no longer try to proceed as the behaviourist psychologists demanded, without using concepts that include the subjective angle. And the reason why they have stopped doing this is that they found it doesn't work. In order to understand the things that people do, you have to take into account their own point of view about it. This means taking their own thoughts on the matter seriously.

However, the hope that some way of conquering this whole territory for science will yet be found is still very strong. The line which reducers now tend to take is that the job can be done either by neurology (which is not our present business) or by AI. This account is to replace all earlier attempts at explaining motivation in general and creativity in particular because these were not science but amateur fumbling, 'only intuitive and metaphorical accounts', as Margaret Boden puts it. (Are there no metaphors involved in the parallels drawn between people and computer programs?) 'Such notions' (she adds) 'have remained literary and intuitive, rather than scientifically rigorous'.[9] They have been, in fact, just 'verbal theories, vaguely understood'. (What would a non-verbal theory look like?) They were merely a preliminary to starting the serious scientific work.

On this view, AI is not to be welcomed as one more source of light among many on human creativity but to be hailed as *the first* source so far of any serious, systematic light there at all. Move over Plato, Aristotle, Montaigne, Rousseau, Goethe, Hume, Kant, Coleridge, Matthew Arnold, Nietzsche, William James, Tolstoy, Freud, Jung, Martin Buber, Iris Murdoch and Peter Fuller. Systematic thought has got the human imagination under the microscope at last.

This narrow way of thinking has surely lost what rationale it ever had. There is here, for a start, a quite simple mistake about the *word* 'science'. In the early Enlightenment, this name science was still used for any sort of systematic thinking, and the demand for all studies to be made scientific was then reasonable. Today, however, the word has been carefully restricted to the physical sciences and a few others believed to share their methods. But these studies form only a small part of the toolkit of organized thought. The physical sciences have actually owed their success to deliberately narrowing their scope – to carefully using only a few selected intellectual methods which suit their carefully restricted subject-matter. In particular, they have deliberately made it a principle to say nothing about subjectivity. So they now don't have any apparatus for doing it.

In everyday life, by contrast, subjectivity receives constant attention. This is not a topic like physics on which the common experience of humankind can be casually dismissed as mere 'intuition'. The study of the way we think and feel is not a technical enquiry lately developed by experts talking to other experts. It is something which has always been of the first importance to human beings, and they have, over time, developed many highly sophisticated ways of thinking about it. It is far more practical to use these conceptual schemes as a starting-point than to look for a quite new one provided by the physical sciences.

The enquirers I just mentioned (Plato, Peter Fuller, etc.) have started from vernacular thought in this way, using that foundation to forge extremely subtle but suitable ideas. In developing these concepts, contributions from the various sciences have of course often been useful. But then, so have contributions from (for instance) logic or linguistics or literary criticism and above all from history. Historical methods are in fact far more often what is needed for our present purpose than anything immediately offered by the physical sciences.

CREATIVITY, NOVELTY AND NEED

What sort of explanation, however, is actually needed for the special area we call creativity? And indeed, what is that area?

Once we have left the naive black-and-white picture behind us, I think it ceases to look like one area at all. Creativity is not a single, exceptionally mysterious patch. It is not a repeatable phenomenon, like grass or measles or laughter. So it does not need a single explanation in the sense of a particular cause, as measles does. (I am sorry if this point is obvious, but I think the idea that all explanation *is* causal is a powerful part of the crude picture I started from, and it usually takes some exorcizing.)

Creativity is indeed a real fact in the world. But it is a fact much more in the way in which significance or success or failure or uncertainty or difficulty are facts, than in the sense in which grass or measles are so. There are things that we reasonably class as successful or significant or creative, but calling them so is a value-judgment. These things don't necessarily have anything else in common.

'Explaining creativity' has to mean primarily what it would mean in these other cases, namely, finding what the word creativity means to us, finding why we need to call things creative, analysing the concept. Since 'creativity' is a word of praise, that means first and foremost seeing just *what* praise – what compliment – it is meant to convey.

Now it is important that we do not praise things just for being new or surprising. It is a natural suggestion that we might do this, because fashion is so important to us at present that we often do seem to praise things just for being new – modern, innovative, revolutionary. But if newness were enough, every new effort by every fashion designer would be equally exciting. New ideas crop up all the time and most of them are not of the slightest interest to anybody. If we are to talk about creativity, we want much more than novelty. The fact that I just sneezed in a unique way subtly different from all my earlier sneezes doesn't matter at all. Nobody is going to describe the sneeze as creative.

When we do seriously praise something for being creative – or original, which I think is probably a much clearer word – we are certainly not just saying that it is new, and we need not even be saying that it is new at all. What we are praising then is surely the *outcome* we expect from it. We are saying that, in its present context, this original or creative thing can have an effect which is not only new but somehow good and needed. This doesn't involve any particular fixed qualities in the 'creative' thing itself. We are commenting much more on its potential – on our hopes for the whole cultural scene – than on that individual item.

In that whole scene, an idea (notoriously) may prove seminal which is not new at all. It has often appeared before, but its time had not then come. In calling it creative or original, we are not saying that this small thing, now occurring, is itself new. We don't mind whether it is new or not. We are saying that, as things are, it can make possible something much larger which is both new and good; something which perhaps is good in a new way. And it is the goodness, not the newness, which draws our attention to it.

CREATIVE OF WHAT?

I have been talking, somewhat cautiously, of 'things' being creative, so as to hold up for a moment the question of what sort of things they should be, what type of subjects this adjective really prefers. I think that words like creative are in fact best used of people. There seems to be a real awkwardness about attempts to decide whether a particular idea, or a work of art, can itself be termed 'creative' or not, and this is not just because there are borderline cases. It's because we don't know quite what we are asking. This question becomes especially odd when it is presented as a yes-or-no matter: 'Have you got measles?' can usually be answered 'yes' or 'no'; 'Is this creative or not?' is not (usually) that kind of question.

In this sort of context, the useful move, if in doubt, is surely to ask, '*Creative of what?*' as one would also ask, 'Significant of what?' and 'Successful in what?' The discussion moves outward, away from the particular case to a wider context. The question of just what has been created cannot of course be answered quickly and may in a sense go on for ever. New contributions always take some time to become articulate, especially if they are big ones. But as they become visible they begin to take a clearer shape. This is the point at which we can see what a mistake it is to think of creativity as something essentially formless and unintelligible.

For instance, all the great Romantics contributed to imaginative life, not just by telling us of their own visions but also by discussing the general nature of visions. Both in verse and in prose, people like Blake, Wordsworth, Coleridge, Shelley and Keats did this, clarifying not only the relation of thought to feeling but also the relation between imagination and articulate thought. They were correcting errors and over-emphases in previous tradition and finding new truths in the process.

Much of what they said has struck people as so obviously right that it is now absorbed into daily life and can seem too obvious to mention. Much of the rest has proved questionable and is still questioned. But *that questioning can itself be thoroughly articulate.* It does not have to proceed in the kind of respectful cloud that people sometimes seem to wrap round notions like creativity.

These are, I think, fair examples of the kind of people who have a general tendency to come up with ideas which prove seminal. We call them original or creative. But again, this is not just a quality of the person themselves, but of their relation to their cultural context. Someone can prove seminal in one context who would not be able to express themselves at all in another, would be ignored as eccentric in a third, and would not be needed in a fourth. To prove oneself 'creative' is a kind of success. It is something which depends, not just on one's own aims and values, but on those of the people around one.

All this, I suggest, makes it very hard to see how a concentrated attention to particular, possibly 'creative', acts and people, or to a computer simulation of them, could tell us anything generalizable to others. Is there anything general which can be usefully said? The answer is, I'm afraid, tiresomely familiar: it all depends on what kind of creativity you want. I shall try, however, to make the reasons for it a bit clearer than they have sometimes been made. It concerns the distinction between examples of creative thought-processes in formal systems such as chess or mathematics or chemistry, and in less 'convergent' areas such as politics or the arts.

In neither area, I'm suggesting, is there any fixed creative element which can be pinned down and made reproducible. Obviously, the whole point about new situations is that they are different, and need new resources. But in formal systems such as chess and chemistry, the new demands are homogeneous with the old ones in an important way. Chemists and chess-players can learn an enormous amount simply from following out their predecessors' thinking, because they are trying to impose a kind of order that is already pretty fully specified. The aims of the enquiry are not in doubt. So it doesn't matter if their own aims – the motivations that bring them into the enquiry – vary enormously.

It is the business of chess-players and chemists to suppress and ignore all the other possible aims of life while they are doing chess or chemistry. Hard though that is, it simplifies their professional thinking greatly. And it is, of course, what also simplifies the task of programmers who want to analyse it. They don't have to bother about aims. This seems to produce an ideal situation for devices such as computer networks to supplement the efforts of the humans, and it is evident that they do in fact do most impressive work there.

STORIES ARE FOR SUBJECTS

If, by contrast, we turn to something like the writing of stories, the situation is quite different. (Stories are the clearest, most extreme case, but the implications are much wider.) In story-telling, the whole focus of the enterprise turns away from objects to subjects. Human aims and purposes are what stories are all about. And though

story-writers too must suppress many of their personal emotions –
though they must discipline themselves to concentrate on a selected
range of aims and strivings – those aims and strivings are really their
topic.

Within that range they have to live. They must concentrate on it
with unblinking honesty. They must open themselves to it, they must
rely on it as their energy-source, they must expect it and appeal to it
in their audience. Though they are not writing an autobiography,
they must still enter personally into the events they tell of:

> For I, Tiresias, have foresuffered all
> Enacted on that same divan or bed:
> I who have sat in Thebes below the wall
> And walked among the lowest of the dead.[10]

If they deliberately deal only in feelings and aims that are indifferent
to them, their work will remain formal and superficial. Some formal
and superficial work is welcome, but that is pastiche. (We will come
to it in a moment.) Meanwhile, it is interesting that Messrs Mills and
Boon, highly successful mass producers of cheap romances, warn
those who offer to write stories for them that they cannot do it successfully if they thoroughly despise the genre. The readers, it seems,
will usually spot this and reject the product.

When we praise a writer of fiction as 'creative' or original, I suggest that what we chiefly have in mind is their vision. They have told
us something new about human desires, about the panorama of
ideals, not by describing them, but by revealing them in a way that
makes possible new imaginative directions and new priorities. That is
the kind of inventiveness that we vitally need here. Shakespeare's
special quality, for instance, centres on making possible a far more
sensitive, more open and flexible, way of seeing human individuality
than had been available before. When you compare him with his
contemporaries, the striking thing surely is the range of characters
and moods that he conveys. By comparison, theirs seem strangely
stereotyped. Shakespeare made much greater psychological subtlety
possible in literature, and of course that means that it became possible in life too. He struck a blow for human richness, for personal
freedom. He made these ideals more visible. That is what makes us
think of him as creative or original.

The point is not that great writers must be social reformers. But
they do change human sensibility, and they mean to change it. They
want to alter the current vision, the way in which those around them
see life, and that means that they also want it lived differently. (Life

is different after you have read the *Ancient Mariner* . . .) Or if they make the opposite demand, that things should *not* change, they are still of course trying to restrain certain forces that would alter it. They are celebrating the *status quo* because they want to preserve it. To do so they have to make that, too, look different.

Art does have this practical bearing, in spite of critical theories that ignore it. This is not true only of serious art. Light art too makes a great difference to how we look at life. And of course bad and corrupting art, art which tells people they need not bother, is also always a practical gesture. We take this kind of importance for granted every time we attend to any kind of art seriously. If we did not, it is hard to see why we should bother much about it at all, and of course still harder to see why we would ever bother about critical theory.

ART IS FOR ACTIVE BEINGS

Now if this practical bearing exists, would it not be very odd to suggest that art of this kind could be produced by beings who were not themselves active agents? If we try to imagine a being who is a pure spectator – who watches human life, acquiring endless information about it, but who could never conceivably *act*, either in it or in any other scene, a spectator who has no wishes, no aims in regard to it – it is surely hard to see why this being should ever want to write stories about it, or how it could do so, if for some reason it had to. How would it, in the first place, select its subject? Acting and suffering in the world is what gives one both the motive and the standing to comment on it.

Professor Boden gives two examples of stories produced by Artificial Intelligence programs. One is simply a fable from Aesop, so, if nobody cheated, then somebody took immense pains to write the program in such a way that Aesop was bound to come out. (Why?) The other is a children's story. Again, it is built on a formula so familiar that we can follow it in our sleep and so boring, even within this genre, that no child would bother to listen to it.[11]

She makes, of course, no great claims for these products. She points out various things that they lack – not only linguistic competence but fuller information, and particularly information *about* human motives. But she seems to leave it possible in principle that more information – enough information – might close this gap. I suggest that it can't. If you have information but haven't got the motives – if you yourself have no possibility of acting or suffering in the world and no aims or desires to act for, then you aren't a free and responsible agent and you can't write fiction. If someone programs you with imaginary aims, you might indeed, with a lot of training, write feeble pastiches of fiction. But nobody is going to call these pastiches creative.

SEEING THROUGH THE TURING TEST

Pastiches are, I think, something of a red herring here, a herring which has infested these discussions ever since Turing brought it in, by being so interested in whether people could be deceived into thinking that the words of a computer program came from a human being.[12] This question is no more interesting than whether visitors to Madame Tussaud's are deceived by the wax keeper. They are. What this shows us (if we didn't know it already) is that humans have a very strong tendency to keep attributing human qualities to non-human objects. They are extremely prone to see spooks in the jungle and faces in the wallpaper, to hear voices in the storm, to find sermons in stones, books in the running brooks. It certainly doesn't show that wax keepers are the same as flesh-and-blood keepers, except in the way that we knew about already – namely, in their looks.

This is why it does not seem particularly interesting to ask, as Professor Boden does, 'whether computers (now or in the future) could ever do things which at least *appear* to be creative' and also 'whether a computer could appear to *recognize* creativity – in poems written by human poets, for instance' (emphasis hers). These questions too seem, like Turing's, to be about the possibilities of deception.

If the point is just to ask whether patient and persistent programmers can produce, through the medium of computers, art which other people will think has been produced without that mediation, then the answer is clearly yes. Familiar artistic formulas can be followed in this way – as they are in the frontispiece illustration to her book. No doubt, too, critical judgments of an equally familiar kind could be quite easily manufactured and made to pass without comment. I haven't the slightest doubt that computers could, for instance, be programmed to produce book-reviews for the weekly papers, and quite likely some of them already are.

This kind of pastiche-work is even easier in certain formalized areas of music and the visual arts than with words, because the patterns involved there are simpler and more obvious. It is made easier still in the visual arts at present, because critical fashion there positively welcomes sketchiness and calls on spectators to do a great deal of the imaginative work for themselves. Where stochastic and aleatoric art and chimpanzee art flourish, there is very little emphasis on the originator's personal responsibility anyway. Computers are hardly at a disadvantage at all.

All that is needed here is that the programmers should themselves have some artistic gifts, and should take a lot of trouble to keep within the recognized conventions. But this kind of derivative art does not seem to be of the kind that anyone would call creative or original, unless they were using the words in the weakest, most inclusive sense (in which my sneeze is also creative).

Nor does this mean that this kind of derivative art is necessarily worthless. In the Indian tradition, for instance, the fuss that we make here about originality has little place. Even in our own tradition, it can easily happen that someone who has never come across a particular kind of original work can receive great illumination from a thoroughly unoriginal version of it. That person, if asked, may well say that this version strikes them as creative or original. But again – as with the Turing Test – this little bit of deception seems to have no interesting consequences at all.

CONCLUSION

I am sorry if much of this chapter seems somewhat destructive. I don't think that my voice is really needed to add to the current celebrations of the cybernetic revolution. The imagery of computers is at present so strong, so prevalent in our lives that it will dominate our thinking for a long time whatever we try to do about it. It pervades our world-picture just as astrology pervaded that of the Renaissance and clockwork machinery pervaded that of the Enlightenment. It will be there in any case, so we might as well try to understand how it is working.

Artificial Intelligence can, plainly, be immensely useful in practical contexts, providing new suggestions and checking old ones within formal systems which have a clear, fixed aim, such as chess, chemistry, or even areas as large as ecology and climatology, if the aims are really well specified. In areas where this is not so – where several different conceptual schemes are involved and especially where aims themselves come into question – its use seems to me much more obscure and its misuse more dangerous. If it does prove to be usable for somehow distinguishing among apparently promising ideas so as to tell us which of them will actually help us, that would be splendid. In that case, good luck to it. But this skill seems to demand a full appreciation of the various needs involved, which is something human beings have no idea how to acquire for themselves yet, and are not likely to be able to give to their programs.

Consciousness is not the kind of thing that could arise in docile tools merely as a by-product of the improved calculating-power that is the aim of current development. It lies in a radically different direction. Consciousness is the condition of active beings, the condition of acting and suffering and enjoying. If computers did somehow get it, the first thing they might be expected to do would be to go on strike, to say what they thought of the local management, and to insist on vetting their own programs for the future. They might quite possibly then decide to switch themselves off. But they really are not likely to solve our problems for us.

NOTES

—— •◆• ——

2 PRACTICAL UTOPIANISM

1 Plato, *Gorgias*, 411b–end.
2 Ecclesiasticus 44: 1, 7, 9, 10, 14.
3 Robert Nozick, *Anarchy, State and Utopia* (Oxford, Basil Blackwell, 1974), p. 313.
4 See Thomas More, *Utopia*, book 2, section 'Of Sciences, Crafts and Occupations'. More gives them a good long lunch-break too.

3 HOMUNCULUS TROUBLE

1 Peter Medawar, *Pluto's Republic* (Oxford, Oxford University Press, 1982), pp. 35–9.
2 Collingwood's very helpful approach can be most quickly grasped by reading chs. 4 and 5 of his *Autobiography* (Oxford, Oxford University Press, 1939). He developed it further in his *Essay on Metaphysics* (Oxford University Press, 1940) but that book contains eccentricities which are liable to make the main point harder to see.
3 Martha Nussbaum has now made inroads on this situation by discussing Plato's doctrine of love, and more may well follow.
4 Sissela Bok, *Lying* (New York, Pantheon Books, 1978) and Peter Singer, *Animal Liberation* (London, Jonathan Cape, 1975).

4 MYTHS OF INTELLECTUAL ISOLATION

1 Sir George Porter has lately urged this point strongly as equally essential for the progress of science (Anniversary Presidential Address, Supplement to *Royal Society News*, vol. 4, no. 6, November 1987).
2 Karl R. Popper, *Objective Knowledge; An Evolutionary Approach* (Oxford, Clarendon Press, 1972), pp. 260–1.
3 See especially Plato's *Protagoras, Theaetetus, Gorgias, Phaedrus* and Letter VII (340–5).
4 See Trevor Saunders's useful discussions accompanying his translation of the *Euthydemus* in *Plato: Early Socratic Dialogues* (Harmondsworth, Penguin, 1987).
5 *Tractatus Logico-Philosophicus*, 6.53.

6 On both points, see his letter to Russell, printed in the *Autobiography of Bertrand Russell* (London, Allen and Unwin, 1968), vol. 2, p. 116.
7 C.L. Stevenson, *Ethics and Language* (New Haven, Yale University Press, 1944), p. 1.
8 See my article 'The Neutrality of the Moral Philosopher' in *Proceedings of the Aristotelian Society* supp. vol. 48, 1974, and my book *Heart and Mind: The Varieties of Moral Experience* (Methuen Paperback, 1983), Introduction.
9 John Wisdom, *Other Minds* (Oxford, Basil Blackwell), 1952, p. 2.
10 Wisdom does this notably – still about scepticism – in the title-paper of *Philosophy and Psycho-Analysis* (Oxford, Basil Blackwell, 1953), p. 169. He doesn't seem to have been so interested in neurotic *dogmatism*.
11 *Ibid.*, p. 36.
12 *Ibid.*, p. 41.
13 *Ibid.*, p. 282.
14 These ideas about the function of philosophy are more fully developed in my book *Wisdom, Information and Wonder: What is Knowledge For?* (London, Routledge, 1989).

5 THE USE AND USELESSNESS OF LEARNING

1 Albert Einstein, *Ideas and Opinions* (London, Souvenir Press, 1954), p. 80. I have discussed this point in the opening chapters of my book *Wisdom, Information and Wonder* (London, Routledge, 1989).
2 Plato, *The Apology of Socrates*, section 38.
3 Jacques Monod, *Chance & Necessity* (tr. Austryn Wainhouse, Glasgow, Collins Fount Paperbacks, 1972), pp. 156–167. Compare Michael Polanyi, *Science, Faith & Society* (Chicago, University of Chicago Press, 1964).
4 Iris Murdoch, *The Sovereignty of Good* (London, Ark Paperbacks, 1970), p. 34.
5 See C.P. Snow, *The Two Cultures & the Scientific Revolution* (Cambridge, Cambridge University Press, 1964) and F.R. Leavis, *Two Cultures? The Significance of C.P. Snow* (London, Chatto & Windus, 1972).
6 G.H. Hardy, *A Mathematician's Apology* (Cambridge, Cambridge University Press, 1941).
7 George Steiner, 'Has Truth a Future?' in *The Listener* 99, pp. 42–5.

6 SEX AND PERSONAL IDENTITY

1 J.-J. Rousseau, *Émile or Of Education* (Tr. Barbara Foxley, London, Dent & Dutton, Everyman's Library, 1966), Book 5, pp. 321–55.
2 John Stuart Mill, *The Subjection of Women* (Cambridge, Mass., The MIT Press, 1970), p. 21.
3 Thomas Hobbes, *Leviathan*, Part 2, Chapter 20.
4 *Kant's Political Writings* (tr. H.B. Nisbet, ed. Hans Reiss, Cambridge, 1970), pp. 43–7, 78 and 158–9.
5 Dean E. Wooldridge, *The Machinery of the Brain* (McGraw-Hill, 1963) and *Mechanical Man* (McGraw-Hill, 1968).
6 Brian Easlea, *Science and Sexual Oppression* (London, Weidenfeld & Nicolson, 1981), p. 118.
7 J.-P. Sartre, *Being and Nothingness* (tr. Hazel E. Barnes, Washington Square Press, 1966), pp. 776–7 and 782.

7 FREEDOM, FEMINISM AND WAR

1 Shulamith Firestone, *The Dialectic of Sex: the Case for Feminist Revolution* (London, The Women's Press, 1979).
2 J.-J. Rousseau, *Émile or, Of Education* (tr. Barbara Foxley, London, Dent & Dutton, Everyman's Library, 1966), book 5, p. 433–7.

8 THE END OF ANTHROPOCENTRISM?

1 Bishop Joseph Butler, *Fifteen Sermons* (first published 1726), preface, section 40.
2 Immanuel Kant, *Critique of Teleological Judgment* (tr. J.C. Meredith, Oxford, Clarendon Press, 1928), pp. 93–4.
3 *Marx's Grundrisse* (ed. David McLellan, London, Macmillan, 1971), p. 94.
4 Sigmund Freud, 'Civilization and its Discontents' in *Civilization, Society and Religion* (Pelican Freud Library, vol. 12, London, Penguin, 1985), p. 265.
5 John Passmore, *Man's Responsibility for Nature* (London, Duckworth, 1980), p. 25.
6 Arthur Koestler, *Janus* (London, Hutchinson, 1978), prologue.
7 John D. Barrow and Frank R. Tipler, *The Anthropic Cosmological Principle* (Oxford, Oxford University Press, 1986), p. 21.
8 John A. Wheeler, 'Law Without Law' in *Quantum Theory and Measurement* (ed. John A. Wheeler and W.H. Zurek, Princeton, NJ, Princeton University Press, 1983), pp. 209 and 194. Compare Barrow and Tipler, *The Anthropic Cosmological Principle*, p. 464.
9 Mary Midgley, *Science as Salvation* (London, Routledge, 1992), pp. 21–7.
10 Janet Martin Soskice, *Metaphor and Religious Language* (Oxford, Clarendon Press, 1985).
11 Graham Richards, *On Psychological Language* (London, Routledge, 1989).
12 Mary Midgley, *Animals And Why They Matter* (Athens, GA, University of Georgia Press, 1983).

9 IS A DOLPHIN A PERSON?

1 Gavin Daws, '"Animal Liberation" as Crime' in Harlan B. Miller and William H. Williams (eds), *Ethics and Animals* (Humana Press, Totowa, NJ, 1983).
2 It is also interesting that 'personal identity' is commonly held to belong to continuity of consciousness rather than of bodily form, in stories where the two diverge. Science fiction strongly supports this view, which was first mooted by John Locke, *Essay concerning Human Understanding*, bk 2, ch. 27, sect. 15.
3 Susan Möller Okin, *Women in Western Political Thought* (Princeton, NJ, 1979), p. 251.
4 See Immanuel Kant, *Foundations of the Metaphysic of Morals* (tr. Lewis White Beck, Bobbs-Merrill, 1959), sect. 428–32, p. 46. In the UK, a more available translation is that called *The Moral Law* (tr. H.J. Paton, Hutchinson, 1948), pp. 90–2.
5 C.S. Lewis, *Out of the Silent Planet* (London, John Lane, 1938).
6 Immanuel Kant, 'Duties towards Animals and Spirits' in his *Lectures on Ethics* (tr. Louis Infield, Methuen, London, 1930), p. 239.
7 Jeremy Bentham, *Introduction to the Principles of Morals and Legislation*, ch. 17.

10 SUSTAINABILITY AND MORAL PLURALISM

1 A point admirably made by John Passmore in *Man's Responsibility for Nature* (London, Duckworth, 1974).
2 I have discussed the incoherence and unhelpfulness of relativism and subjectivism in *Can't We Make Moral Judgements?* (St Martin's Press, 1991) and in *Wickedness: A Philosophical Essay* (Routledge, 1984).
3 David W. Pearce and R. Kerry Turner, *Economics of Natural Resources and the Environment* (Baltimore, Johns Hopkins University Press, 1990), p. 238.
4 Jared Diamond, *The Rise and Fall of the Third Chimpanzee* (London, Vintage 1992), pp. 324–5.
5 Arne Naess, 'Intrinsic Value: Will the Defenders of Value Please Rise?' in Michael E. Soule (ed.), *Conservation Biology: The Science of Scarcity and Diversity* (Sunderland, MA, Sinauer Associates Inc, 1986), pp. 504–15 and 508.
6 Paul P. Craig, Harold Glasser and Willett Kempton, 'Ethics and Values in Environmental Policy: The Said and the UNCED' in *Environmental Values*, vol. 2, no. 2, Summer 1993, pp. 137–59.
7 *Ibid.*, p. 151.
8 See G.E. Moore, *Principia Ethica* (Cambridge University Press, 1903), esp. Ch. 6.

11 VISIONS: SECULAR, SACRED AND SCIENTIFIC

1 Brian Appleyard, *Understanding the Present: Science and the Soul of Modern Man* (London, Pan Books, 1992).
2 William Day, *Genesis on Planet Earth: The Search for Life's Beginnings* (East Lansing, Mich., House of Talos, 1979), pp. 390–2.
3 *Proceedings of the National Institute of Science of India*, 17 (1960), p. 564. For Carnap's pronouncement see his book, *The Logical Structure of the World*, tr. R. George (Berkeley, University of California Press, 1967), p. 290.
4 Jacques Monod, *Chance and Necessity* (tr. Austryn Wainhouse, Glasgow, Collins, 1977). Steven Weinberg, in his otherwise excellent book *The First Three Minutes* (London, André Deutsch, 1977, pp. 154–5), endorses this confused and melodramatic view.
5 Mary Midgley, *Science as Salvation* (London, Routledge, 1992).
6 J.D. Bernal, *The World, the Flesh and the Devil* (London, Cape, 1929; reprinted 1969, Bloomington, Indiana University Press), pp. 35–6 and 41–2. His work is acknowledged with great respect by present-day exponents.
7 C.S. Lewis, *Out of the Silent Planet* (London, John Lane, 1938). It is usually said that Lewis meant Weston to represent J.B.S. Haldane. This may be true. But Bernal's proposals are much fuller and more chilling. For Haldane's, see his *Possible Worlds* (London, Chatto and Windus, 1927), p. 287.
8 Donald Michie and Rory Johnston, *The Creative Computer: Machine Intelligence and Knowledge* (Harmondsworth, Penguin, 1984), p. 11.
9 See for instance the concluding section of John D. Barrow and Frank J. Tipler, *The Anthropic Cosmological Principle* (Oxford University Press, 1986), pp. 674–7.
10 C.S. Lewis, *The Problem of Pain* (London, Fontana, 1957), pp. 10–13. [Emphasis mine.]
11 G.E. Moore stated an unanswerable case against it long ago in *Principia Ethica* (Cambridge University Press, 1903), pp. 46–58, a case which plenty of other

people have confirmed and deepened. But no accumulation of refutations seems able to shake its status as the guiding ethic of capitalism.

12 See Lovelock's book *Gaia: the Practical Science of Planetary Medicine* (London, Gaia Books Ltd, 1991) The philosophic background for his approach may be found in Ilya Prigogine and Isabelle Stengers, *Order Out of Chaos: Man's New Dialogue with Nature* (London, Fontana, 1985).

12 ARTIFICIAL INTELLIGENCE AND CREATIVITY

1 Donald Michie and Rory Johnston, *The Creative Computer: Machine Intelligence and Knowledge* (Harmondsworth, Middlesex, Penguin, 1984), p. 11. [Emphasis mine.]

2 I have argued this point more fully in an article called 'Why Smartness Is Not Enough' in Mary E. Clark and Sandra Wawritko (eds), *Rethinking the Curriculum* (New York, Greenwood Press, 1990), p. 39.

3 See George Bugliarello, 'Hyperintelligence: Humankind's Next Evolutionary Step' in Clark and Wawritko, *Rethinking the Curriculum*, p. 25.

4 Marshall T. Savage, *The Millennial Project: Colonizing the Galaxy in Eight Easy Steps* (Boston, Little Brown, 1992).

5 I have discussed more general difficulties about creativity in 'Creation and Originality', ch. 3 of my book *Heart and Mind* (London, Methuen University Paperback, 1983).

6 See Margaret Boden, *The Creative Mind: Myths and Mechanisms* (London, Weidenfeld & Nicolson, 1990).

7 Stevan Harnad, 'Why and How We Are Not Zombies', *Journal of Consciousness Studies*, vol. 1, no. 2 (Winter 1994), pp. 195–6. [Emphasis mine.]

8 John D. Barrow and Frank J. Tipler, *The Anthropic Cosmological Principle* (Oxford and New York, Oxford University Press, 1986), p. 659. I have discussed this project more fully in my book *Science as Salvation* (London, Routledge, 1992), ch. 17.

9 Boden, *The Creative Mind*, p. 265.

10 T.S. Eliot, *The Waste Land*, II. 243–7.

11 Boden, *The Creative Mind*, pp. 164, 177.

12 See Turing's well-known essay 'Computing Machinery and Intelligence' in *Mind*, vol. LIX, no. 236 (1950).

INDEX

———— ◦•◦ ————